THE LIFE OF JOHN MYTTON

Drawn and Etched by T. J. Rawlins and H. Alken

"Well done, Nick, or Nothing!
You are not a bad one to breed from."

MEMOIRS OF THE LIFE OF THE LATE JOHN MYTTON, Esq.

OF HALSTON, SHROPSHIRE, FORMERLY M.P. FOR SHREWSBURY, HIGH SHERIFF FOR THE COUNTIES OF SALOP AND MERIONETH, AND MAJOR OF THE NORTH SHROPSHIRE YEOMANRY CAVALRY; WITH NOTICES OF HIS HUNTING, SHOOTING, DRIVING, RACING, ECCENTRIC AND EXTRAVAGANT EXPLOITS

BY

NIMROD

WITH NUMEROUS ILLUSTRATIONS BY
HENRY ALKEN AND T. J. RAWLINS

METHUEN & CO. LTD. LONDON
36 *Essex Street*, *W*.*C*.2

NOTE

THIS Issue is founded on the Second Edition, printed by Rudolph Ackermann in the year 1837 (with considerable additions) from the NEW SPORTING MAGAZINE

First Published by Methuen & Co., May 1903
Reprinted October 1903, January 1904
September 1906 and July 1910

Sixth Edition . . . . *February 1915*
Seventh Edition . . . . *May 1919*
Eighth Edition (*Small Crown 8vo*) *1936*

PRINTED IN GREAT BRITAIN

PREFACE

BISHOP BURNETT'S narrative of the remarkable passages in the life of the very celebrated Earl of Rochester has been greatly valued, not only as an elegant composition, but as a lesson of instruction to all mankind. The latter of these honours, to a certain extent, I may venture to claim as the result of this sketch—at all events such is, in part, its design; and as no subject is so interesting to man as man, I have a good theme for my pen, inasmuch as there is one present to my mind whose equal, as a private English gentleman, the world never before saw, neither is it, for some reasons, desirable the world should ever again see. My only fear is, that I may be deficient in strength of pencil to draw the picture to the life, and to represent the anomaly in human nature which the character of the late John Mytton presents; at one time, an honour to his nature; at another, a satire on humanity. What more can be done, than to strike the balance with an even hand? and as the brightness of the sun hides its blemishes, let me hope the greater part of his faults will be lost amidst the virtues with which they are mingled. At all events, my purpose is not to hold up the torch to the failings of my old and never-forsaken friend—*my chief object being to account for them*, and leave his virtues to speak for themselves. I owe him pity on the score of human nature; he claims it by his own acts and deeds; and, above all, by one act of Him to whose will all men must bow, and by whom all men's deeds will be weighed. Let not the lash of censure, then, fall too heavy upon one who himself carried charity to excess! Let the greatness of his fall be unto him as a shield; let it be remembered he died in a prison, an epitome of human misery! A glance over his history, however, may not be unprofitable; it will "point a moral," if it do not "adorn a tale."

But it may be objected that I am not the person fitted to perform this task; for, "where is the man," says Johnson, "who can confine himself to the exact balance of justice when his own feelings are unwittingly thrown into the scale?" It is true my regard for the late Mr. Mytton was won and secured by many sterling acts of kindness and friendship; and it is also true, that friendship is not *always* the sequel of obligation. I am proud to assert I do not come within this exception; and pledging myself to saying nothing that is false, rather than all that is true, I think I can produce these two results:—First, I shall unload the memory of a man I shall never be ashamed to call my friend, of several weighty imputations which now rest upon it unjustly; and secondly, I shall show, that the boldest efforts of the human imagination cannot much exceed the romance of real life.

NIMROD

Calais, 1835

CONTENTS

PART I. 1

Pedigree of Mr. Mytton—His original name—His contest for the county of Salop—His ancestor Thomas Mytton—Halston described—Extent of Mr. Mytton's property, and its various situations—His education—Why called Mango—Enters the army—His doings at Calais when in the 7th Hussars—His first marriage—His sister, her character—His person and mind described—His pugnacious disposition—His dress—His method of following wildfowl—His feats in riding the road, and his walking—His powers of digestion—His daring exploits, putting his life to hazard—Upsets a friend in a gig—His wonderful escapes in carriages—His indifference to pain—Is taken for a tailor with Lord Derby's hounds—His treatment of a Jew money-lender—His extraordinary frolics with his chaplain, his doctor, a bear, a horse-dealer, a filly in training, dogs, foxes, &c. — An evening at Halston—His contest with a ferocious dog—His reason for selling an old family estate—His general character—His establishment at Halston—Amount of his expenditure—His fox-hounds, his racing establishment, his game preserves, his cellars, and his wardrobe—" Light come, light go "—His gambling—Only one John Mytton—His bill for pheasants, &c.—The Halston Chaplain, his character, his death.

PART II. 55

With whom compared—His amours—His popularity, and its rapid decline—His excessive drinking, and its influence on his character and health—His toilette—His generous conduct towards his mother—His philanthropy carried to excess—His talents—His last contest for the borough of Shrewsbury — A capital electioneering squib relating to the same—His politics—His farming —His timber—His planting—As a sportsman—As a horseman—His shooting—His racing—His race-horse Euphrates—His cups—His start and progress on the Turf—His handsome conduct towards his jockey—His second marriage—His conduct in the marriage state—As a husband, and a father—His autograph.

PART III. 119

The breaking up of his establishment at Halston—His arrival at Calais, and his extraordinary proceedings whilst there—Nearly loses his life by setting fire to his shirt to frighten away the hiccup—His mind becomes disordered by his

CONTENTS

sufferings—Extraordinary scenes witnessed by his attendants—Drinks eau de Cologne—Gets better and goes into the country with the Author—Gets quite well, but relapses into his habits of dissipation—Is removed to England, and hence his death warrant—Visits Halston, and thrown into Shrewsbury jail—His conduct there, and his former relation to the jailer—Removed to the King's Bench—Released, and returns to Calais with a female—His extraordinary self-introduction to her—Their arrival together at Calais—His most extraordinary proceedings whilst there—His return to England—His melancholy death in the Bench—His funeral—His will—Reflections on the same by the Author—His Epitaph by ditto.

PART IV. 175

The Author's allusion to a second edition of Mr. Mytton's Life—By whom some of the additional anecdotes have been furnished to him—Mr. Mytton's extraordinary feats on horseback—His frolics—With waggon horses—With a bag fox—With skates—With rats on the ice—With herons—With a badger—With foxes in the bar of an inn at his election for the county of Salop—With a broken-kneed horse, and an old woman—With a flannel petticoat—With his chaplain on his road to church—With a horse-breaker—With a Shrewsbury tradesman—His row at a hell—His extraordinary shooting with a rifle—Extraordinary performances after hounds—Swimming the river Severn, &c.—Marvellous exploit in a tandem by moonlight—Ditto in a gig with the Author—His gig carried over Halston lodge gate—A parallel instance to it at Wrexham—Sale of sporting implements at Halston—Heron shooting—The Shavington Day; "Now for the honour of Shropshire!"—Description of the racing stakes at ditto—Number of the stakes and plates won—Monody on his death, by Tom Moody.

LIST OF THE PLATES

No		PAGE
TITLE. 1.	—" Well done, Neck or Nothing; you are not a bad one to breed from ".	188
2.	—A Nick, or the nearest way home	6
3.	—Wild duck shooting	17
4.	—" What! never upset in a gig ? ".	21
5.	—" I wonder whether he is a good timber-jumper!"	22
6.	—The " Meet " with Lord Derby's staghounds	25
7.	—" Stand and deliver "	26
8.	—" Tally ho! Tally ho!" a new hunter.	27
9.	—The Oaks filly	30
10.	—"Light come, light go"	42
11.	—On Baronet clears nine yards of water.	82
12.	—" D—n this hiccup! ".	127
13.	—A h—ll of a row in a hell. Mytton shows fight.	186
14.	—Swims the Severn at Uppington Ferry.	188
15.	—How to cross a country comfortably after dinner.	190
16.	—Heron shooting: a cooler after a big drink.	197

LIST OF THE PLATES

No.		PAGE
TITLE. 17.	—"A Squire trap, by Jove! A little more and I should have done it"	201
18.	—"Now for the honour of Shropshire." The Shavington Day; a trial of rival packs, and consequently of rival horsemen	201

THE LIFE AND DEATH

OF THE LATE

JOHN MYTTON, Esq.

OF HALSTON, SHROPSHIRE

FORMERLY M.P. FOR SHREWSBURY; HIGH SHERIFF FOR THE COUNTIES OF SALOP AND MERIONETH, AND MAJOR OF THE NORTH SHROPSHIRE YEOMANRY CAVALRY

PART I

"Ubi plura nitent."—Hor.

IT may be unnecessary, perhaps, to go beyond *five* centuries back for the pedigree of John Mytton. No one, I believe, ever doubted his being quite thoroughbred. In fact, no half-bred one could have done much more than half what he did in the space of his short life; but, as I have before said of him, "*nil violentum est perpetuum*"—"'tis the pace that kills," and he was no exception to the rule. It having, however, been stated in the newspaper accounts of his decease, that he had represented the ancient borough of Shrewsbury in Parliament, I shall merely show that, if the ancient relation of his family to a town of which their ancestors had been inhabitants and burgesses upwards of five centuries—in addition to their ample estates in its immediate neighbourhood—*still* goes for any thing, who had a better right to the honour than he had? Looking back into the history of Shrewsbury, we find the borough to have been thus represented :—

A. D. 1373 (reign of Edward III.). Reginold de Mutton (Mutton was the original name) and Richard de Pontesbury, members.
1377. Reginold de Mutton and William de Longenolne, members.
1472. Thomas Mutton and John Hord, members.
1491. William Mutton and Lawrence Hosyer, members.
1520. Edmund Cole and Adam Mutton, members.
1529. Adam Mutton and Robert Dudley, members.
1554. Thomas Mytton (now first so called) and Nicholas Purcell, members.
1690. Richard Mytton and Hon. Andrew Newport, members.
1698. Richard Mytton and John Kynaston, members.
1701. Ditto   ditto   ditto.
1702. Ditto   ditto   ditto.

LIFE OF MYTTON

1705. Richard Mytton and John Kynaston, members.
1710. Ditto and Edward Cresset, Esq., ditto.[1]
1734. John Mytton, grandfather to the subject of this memoir, stood a severe contest for the Borough, but was defeated by Sir Richard Corbet, Bart., and William Kynaston, Esq.; and the late John Mytton, Esq., was elected member, January 14, 1819, having been opposed by Panton Corbet, Esq., who soon resigned the contest. Numbers—Mytton, 384; Corbet, 287.

In so highly an aristocratic county as Shropshire, and one celebrated for its electioneering contentions, these extracts may be sufficient to exhibit the parliamentary pretensions of this ancient family, and of my late departed friend.

In 1480, Thomas Mytton was high sheriff for Shropshire, and apprehended the Duke of Buckingham, who had rebelled against Richard the Third, and conducted him to Salisbury, where, as his historian

[1] This election was the result of a very severe contest. The following was the final state of the poll:—Mytton, 224; Edward Cresset (ancestor of Cresset Pelham, Esq., late M.P. for the county), 222; Thomas Jones (ancestor of Sir Tyrwhitt Jones, Bart), 177; Sir Edward Leighton, Bart., 131.

relates, he was instantly tried, condemned, and executed according to the summary method practised in those ages. His reward for this very important service is recorded in the Harleian MSS., No. 433; in which is an abstract of the Letters Patent, whereby " King Richard the Third grants to his trusty and well-beloved Squire, Thomas Mytton, and to his heirs male, the Castle and Lordship of Cawes, and all appurtenances thereto, amounting to the value of fifty pounds, and late belonging to our rebel and traitor, the late Duke of Buckingham." This Thomas Mytton married one of the daughters of Sir John Burgh, and was an immediate ancestor of the subject of this memoir.

As has been shown, the first conspicuous ancestor of this family was, Reginold de Mutton, of Weston Lizard, Shropshire, now represented through the Wilbrahams and Newports by the present Earl of Bradford; and it is in 1549 that we first find it seated at Halston, when Sir Robert Townsend is stated to have rented Mr. Mytton's large mansion at Cotow, he—Mr. Mytton—having removed to his more recent purchase at Halston—or, as it was then called, *Holy Stone*, much celebrated in history as the scene of bloody deeds in the reign of the first Richard. At this ancient mansion there was a preceptory of Knights Templars, and afterwards of the Knights Hospitallers, under a grant from Queen Elizabeth (who confirmed the alienation of the property from the Knights of St. John of Jerusalem, to whom it was given by an Earl of Arundel who possessed it after the Norman conquest), when purchased, or rather exchanged for, by Edward Mytton of Habberley. There was also formerly an abbey in the village of Halston, taken down more than a century ago; but there is the church or chapel of Halston now standing on the domain, exempt from Episcopal jurisdiction, and without any other revenue than what the Chaplain may be allowed by the owner of it.

Having described ancient, I proceed to modern Halston; and, unless very fastidious indeed, my readers will agree with me in thinking that it ought to satisfy the desires of every moderate man. In the first place, its location is good. Away from any great road, it is within easy reach of two—the London and Holyhead, and the Shrewsbury and Chester — without being subjected to the inconvenience of either; and the lodge-gates open upon an excellent cross turnpike-road, leading from Oswestry to Ellesmere—distant, three miles from the former town and five from the latter. Being situated on a flat, the domain is deprived of some of the advantages the extremely beautiful country by which it is surrounded affords, but still the *tout ensemble* is good. In the front of the mansion is a lawn of about sixty acres of prettily diversified grass-land, and behind it is a tastily laid-out flower garden, contiguous to a fine tract of meadow land separated from it by a deeply sunken fence; and a noble sheet of water, with the old family chapel at the head of it, gives a good finish to the landscape. When I say that the oak is the weed of that part of our island, I scarcely need add that, in a domain of such antiquity as Halston, it is—I fear I must write *was*—to be seen in its full majesty of form; and no estate in the county could produce finer oaks than those which adorned the Halston woods. I can indeed speak to the fact of one which was cut down, about eight years back, containing ten tons of timber, without top or lop! The plantations also, all made by the late Mr. Mytton and to the extent of three miles, nearly encircle the domain, and afford shelter to the superfluity of game which it was his ambition to possess.

The mansion house, without pretensions to magnificence, is replete with every comfort and convenience for a country gentleman's establishment; and is much more commodious than it appears to be, from the offices being for the most part detached. It contains

Drawn and Etched by H. Alken and T. J. Rawlins

A mile, or the nearest way home.
(With the back View of Histon House)

a hall in which there was a billiard table, with a library on one side and Mr. Mytton's dressing-room on the other; and an excellent dining- and two drawing-rooms, connected with each other by double doors, complete the down-stairs suite. There also *was* — oh! I write that word with sorrow—a small but excellent collection of pictures, which the catalogue of them showed had been collected with great care, as ornaments to these, now naked, walls; and a thousand guineas were offered, in my presence, for one of them,[1] but nobly refused by the owner of it. The gardens are most excellent, and, to complete the sketch of this, to me, sort of earthly paradise, there is in the grounds surrounding the house, not only a rookery, but a heronry—very rare in that part of the world —and every description of shooting and fishing that the follower of such sports could require. The surrounding country is also quite upon a par with the "*provincials*"—if not better than most— for either fox-hounds or harriers.

The property of the late Mr. Mytton has been a good deal exaggerated, both as regards the annual value of his estates and the sum accumulated in his minority, which was to the extent of seventeen years. I have good reason to believe that the former (though it

[1] Joseph escaping from Potiphar's wife.

increased afterwards) was under ten thousand a year, and that the latter amounted to about £60,000. Independently of the Halston and Habberly estates, which are in entail, there were three other properties in Shropshire, and one in North Wales of about £800 per annum, with a manor and right of free warren, each very rare in the Principality, and the latter very rare everywhere; but, alas, they are lost in the general wreck. The Welch domain will be described when I touch on the subject of shooting.

Having done with the mansion, we will now proceed to the proprietor of it, who, being born on the 30th of Sept. 1796, was left fatherless before he was two years old; and, as if there was a disposition in his predecessors to drop into an early grave, neither his great grandfather nor his grandfather lived to see a son come of age. As I can only just remember the father of the late Mr. Mytton, I am unable to estimate, in this individual instance, the loss of a father to a son, in his infant state; but in most cases, with heirs to large estates, it is irreparable. It is written of the Gracchi, that they were educated "*non tam in gremio quam in sermone matris*";[1]

---

[1] It is difficult to render this passage literally; but it implies that the Gracchi were not only nursed, but in part educated, by their mother.

and, although it is not every mother that is a Sempronia, their history informs us they were very little the better for it, if not a great deal the worse. We cannot marvel at this. When the plant is young and tender a gentle force will incline it to whichsoever way we may wish, but ere it has even attained its full growth it very unwillingly bends to our hand, and thus is it with human kind. The excessive tenderness of a fond mother is no match for the wayward temper of a darling boy, and how often is his ruin to be traced to this source! In the weakness of her affection she is unable to say "no"; and she only finds out when it is too late, that the object of her affection will neither bridle his passions nor restrain his actions at her bidding; nor indeed, as was unfortunately the case with the memorable subject of this memoir, at that of any other human being. But was not such always the case? The Lacedæmonian lawgiver, at all events, was of this opinion, when he ordered the two hounds to be brought into court to illustrate his argument in favour of moral restraint. One took after a hare and the other ran to his dinner, as each had, in his youth, been instructed to do. "There,' said the Spartan, "is the effect of early discipline; those animals were whelps of the same litter, but the difference of education has made one a good hound, that seldom misses his game, whereas his brother

is a cur, fit for nothing but to lick the dishes."
And thus it is in the stable :—

> " Fingit equum tenerâ docilem cervice magister
> Ire viam, quam monstrat eques "—

writes Horace, when he shows that the temper of
the horse depends upon his treatment when a colt.

It is scarcely necessary for me to observe that,
before he was ten years old, Master Mytton was
as finished a Pickle as the fondest mother and his
own will could possibly have made him. Indeed
his neighbour, Sir Richard Puleston, with a felicity
of expression peculiarly his own, christened him
Mango, the king of the Pickles, and he proved
his title to the honour even to the end of his life.
But Master Mytton was withal a wonderful
favourite in his neighbourhood, because all his
actions were tempered with kindness, as indeed they
were to his very last hour. But how am I to
describe the whole career of his infant state, his
scholastic progress, and his academical honours?
Why the task is performed in a few words.
He was expelled Westminster[1] and Harrow;
knocked down his private tutor in Berkshire, in
whose hands he was afterwards placed; was
entered on the books of both universities, but did

[1] Here he spent £800 a year, exactly double his allowance

not matriculate at either, and the only outward and visible sign of his ever intending to do so, was his ordering three pipes of Port wine to be sent addressed to him at Cambridge. At the age of eighteen, however, he went a tour on the Continent by way of something like "the Finish"; and then returned to Halston, and his harriers which he had kept when he was a child.

But we will now look on him when a man! As the proud recollections of the Roman fathers often disturbed the dreams of their sons, it is possible that our hero, although I never heard him speak of him, might have cherished the recollection of the renowned General Mytton, and wished to signalize himself as he had done, in arms. Be this as it may, at the age of nineteen, he entered, as a Cornet, the 7th Hussars, and joined them in France, with the army of occupation. But as by this time all fighting was at end, Cornet Mytton made himself signal in sundry other ways. A heavy purse and an open hand are by no means necessary qualifications in a soldier; and it was very unlikely that he, above all men, having only a few months to wait for being in full possession of his property, should keep without the magic circle, and not enter into all kinds of youthful mischief. Some of his feats were of a nearly harmless nature, such as his racing exploits—himself the jockey; his borrowing £3,000 of a banker at St. Omer, one day, and losing half of it the next at a rascally E. O. table, which he demolished to atoms as some satisfaction for his loss; but his doings at Calais at this period were of a more serious nature. He lost the immense sum of sixteen thousand Napoleons to a certain Captain, at billiards, which sum he could not then pay. But the score was wiped off in a more agreeable manner. It being suspected to have been a cross, which no doubt it was, the Colonel of his regiment, the Marquess of Anglesea, then Earl of Uxbridge, forbad his paying the money, and with any other man but John Mytton, such authority would have been *conclusive*. He, however, afterwards entered into correspondence with his opponent, which led to the publication of pamphlets and placards; but a late transaction, in which that person's conduct has been implicated, proved how right Lord Anglesea was in his decision, and how wrong the victim was in ever holding a communication with his destroyer.

Quitting the army, and in his twenty-third year, he entered, for the first time, into the marriage state, and his wedding was thus announced in the Shrewsbury papers:—

"On the 21st May, 1818, at St George's Hanover-square, by the Rev. William Douglas, Prebend of Westminster, John Mytton, of Halston, in this county, Esq., to Harriet Emma Jones, eldest daughter of the late Sir Tyrwhitt Jones, Bart., of Stanley-hall, in this county, and sister to the present Sir Tyrwhitt Jones, Bart. The bridegroom was attended by the Earl of Uxbridge, the Earl of Denbigh, Sir Watkin Williams Wynn, Bart., Colonel Sir Edward Kerrison, &c. &c. After the ceremony they returned to the house of Lady Jones, in New Norfolk-street, where a most elegant breakfast was provided; and from thence the happy couple immediately left London for the seat of the Duke of Marlborough, at Blenheim. Among the company present were the Duchess of Marlborough and Lady Caroline Churchill, Sir John and Lady Dashwood and Miss Dashwood, Sir Edward and Lady Kerrison, Lord and Lady Say and Sele and Miss Twisleton, General and Mrs. Gascoyne and Miss Gascoyne, the Marquess of Blandford and Lord Charles Churchill, Mr., Mrs., and Miss Leigh, Sir Tyrwhitt Jones, Mr. and Mrs. Patton Bold and the Misses Bold, and many other persons of distinction."

The issue of this marriage was only one daughter, at present alive, and residing with Mrs. Corbet, of

Sundorne-castle, Shropshire, widow of the ever to be revered John Corbet, who so many years hunted Warwickshire. Mrs. Mytton, whose state of health was always delicate, died a few years after her marriage. Mr. Mytton had but one sister, who was married to John Hesketh Lethbridge, Esq., eldest son of Sir Thomas Lethbridge, Bart., in March, 1817, and she ceased to exist in the same month of the year 1826, leaving two sons and four daughters. She was not only truly elegant in her person, but very highly accomplished, and of a singularly mild and amiable disposition; and those who wish for a confirmation of the eulogium I have passed upon her, may satisfy themselves by referring to the "Gentleman's Magazine," for October, 1826, page 357; where her character is very faithfully sketched in some lines from the pen of a female friend, a niece to the present Bishop of Norwich. Mytton had a great respect for this amiable sister, but would never take her advice, nor indeed that of any living soul.

Both in person, and in mind, the gifts of nature were amply bestowed upon the late Mr. Mytton. In fact, he possessed what are called the animal faculties to a degree seldom witnessed, and had he been commonly temperate in his mode of living, he might, barring accidental death, have attained a very advanced age. The biceps muscle of his arm was larger than that of Jackson's, the celebrated pugilist's, and those of every other part of his body were equally exuberant and powerful. Unfortunately, however, for himself, and often so for his companions, he was, like Cleanthes of old, proud of displaying his strength; but fortunately for mankind he would not, like Cleanthes, be instructed in the art of boxing, or he would have been still more formidable with his fists. As it was, in a "turn up," he was, what is called, a very awkward customer, and when he could get at him he knocked down his man as if he had been a nine-pin. But he was nearly ignorant of the science of self-defence, and, as I have already observed, never attempted to attain it. His bull-dog courage, however, added to his tremendous blow, enabled him to beat any ordinary man; and so well was his prowess known, that few ventured to encounter him. He had not a handsome face, but by no means an unpleasing countenance; and, without having practised the graces, the air and character of the gentleman were strongly impressed on his carriage. His shoulders were finely formed, with a very expanded chest —height, about five feet nine inches; weight, varying in the last twelve years of his life from eleven to thirteen stone.

I should think the best battle he ever fought was in 1826, with a countryman—a Welch miner—who offended him by holloaing the harriers of Mr. Nicholls, of Crumpwell, near Oswestry, to a fresh hare, when they were on the scent of the hunted one, and on the point of killing her after an extraordinary run. The miner told him he would find him "a tough un," which he did; but after twenty rounds he cried, "hold hard, *enough.*" And now appears Mytton in his true character. The hunted hare being eventually killed, he gave the miner ten shillings, told him to go to Halston and get "*another* bellyfull," and to order the hare to be cooked for dinner that day.

Never was constitution so murdered as Mr. Mytton's was; for, what but one of adamant could have withstood the shocks, independent of wine, to which it was almost daily exposed? His dress alone would have caused the death of nine hundred of a thousand men who passed one part of the day and night in a state of luxury and warmth. We will take him from the sole of his shoe to the crown of his hat. He never wore any but the thinnest and finest silk stockings, with very thin boots or shoes, so that in winter he rarely had dry feet. To flannel he was a stranger, since he left off his petticoats. Even his hunting

Drawn and Etched by H. Aiken

Myton wild duck shooting.

breeches were without lining; he wore one small waistcoat, always open in the front from about the second of the lower buttons; and about home he was as often without his hat as with one. His winter shooting gear was a light jacket, white linen trousers, without lining or *drawers, of which he knew not the use*; and in frost and snow he waded through all water that came in his way. Nor is this all. He would sometimes strip to his shirt to follow wild-fowl in hard weather, and once actually laid himself down on the snow in his shirt only to wait their arrival at dusk. But Dame Nature took offence at this, and chastised him rather severely for his daring. On one occasion, however, he out-heroded Herod, for he followed some ducks "*in puris naturalibus*"—anglice, stark-naked—on the ice,[1] and escaped with perfect impunity. He was the only man I ever knew who I think, at one time of his life, might have stood some chance of performing the grand Osbaldeston match over Newmarket, from the ease with which he performed immense distances on the road on his hacks. When his hounds hunted the Albrighton country (Staffordshire) he used to ride, several times in the week, to covers nearly fifty miles

[1] This occurred at Woodhouse, the seat of his uncle, who related the story to me in London, the circumstance having occurred since I last visited Shropshire.

distant from Halston, and return thither to his dinner. Indeed he has been known to do it for some days successively. Neither could any man I ever met in the field walk through the day with him, *at his pace.* I saw him, on his own moors in Merionethshire, completely knock up two keepers (who accompanied him alternately), being the whole day bare-headed under a hot sun. (One of these keepers —whom I procured for him in Cheshire—was rather a crack walker, and a noted man with his fists.) He had the stomach of an ostrich before it was debilitated by wine, and even against that it stood nearly proof to the last, but it appears he once met with his match. Himself and a friend left London together with eighteen pounds of filbert-nuts in his carriage, and they devoured them all before they arrived at Halston. To use his own words, they sat up to their knees in nut-shells. But it was often alarming to witness the quantity of dry nuts he would eat, with the quantity of port wine which he would drink; and on *my* once telling him at his own table that the ill-assorted mixture caused the death of a schoolfellow of mine,[1] he carried a dish of filberts

---

When mentioning this fact, I was quite unconscious that General Williams, who was present, was brother to the youth I alluded to. "You are speaking of a brother of mine," said the General. "Volat irrevocabile verbum;" I had nothing left but to apologize.

into the drawing-room with him, for the purpose of "clearing decks," as he said. Among other peculiarities, he never carried a pocket-handkerchief, for he never had occasion for the use of one; he very rarely wore gloves, for his hands were never cold; and although he never wore a watch, he always knew the hour.

On the subject of nuts, the following anecdote has been handed to me by a gentleman who vouched for the truth of it. Mytton, in his prosperity, was a great favourite of the shopkeepers of Shrewsbury and Oswestry, and among others, of a sporting hair-dresser of the former place, to whom he often gave a day's shooting. This person was his chief purveyor of filberts, and having an unlimited order for the purchase of them, declared that, in one season, he sent to Halston *as many as two cart-loads of them!* As may be supposed, in return for pheasants and hares, the house or shop of Monsieur le Perruquier was now and then the scene of a "lark." Entering it one evening, he asked what he could have to drink? but before an answer could be given him, he snatched up a pint bottle of lavender water, and, knocking off the head of it, drank it off at a draught—saying, "It was a good preservative against the bad effects of night air." I shall presently show that this was not his last performance upon this stage.

That John Mytton saw his thirty-eighth year, must be attributed either to the good genius that accompanied him, or to the signal interposition of Providence, for scarcely a day passed over his head in which he did not put his life to the hazard. Some of his escapes, indeed, border closely on the miraculous, but it would fill a volume were I to enumerate them. How often has he been run away with by horses, in gigs! How often struggling in deep water, without being able to swim! How was it that he did not get torn to pieces in the countless street-broils in which he was engaged;[1] and lastly, how did he avoid being shot in a duel? The latter question is soon answered—*he never fought one.* In fact, he was always considered somewhat of a man of license in society, and although no one doubted his standing fire, if called upon, it is my firm persuasion nothing would have induced him to have aimed at a man to destroy him.

[1] In the literal sense of the term, he was once nearly *divided* into two John Myttons, at a race meeting in Lancashire, for which offence—as well as an attempt to rob him—one man was transported. One party of thieves wanted to pull him *into* a house and the other *out* of it, so between both he was nearer being quartered than divided, and nothing but the great strength of his frame saved him.

Drawn and Etched by H. Alken

What! never upset in a gig?

In the saddle, too, he ran prodigious risks for his life, not only by riding at apparently impracticable fences, with hounds, but in falling from his horses when intoxicated. For the former of these acts he was for many years so notorious, that it was a common answer to the question—whether a certain sort of fence could be leaped, or whether any man would attempt it?—*that it would do for Mytton.* He once actually galloped at full speed over a rabbit-warren, to try whether or not his horse would fall, which of course he did, and rolled over him. This perfect contempt of danger was truly characteristic of himself; but, not content with the possession of it, he endeavoured to impart it to his friends. As he was one day driving one of them in a gig, who expressed a strong regard for his neck, with a hint that he considered it in some danger, Mytton addressed him thus:—"Was you ever much hurt then, by being upset in a gig?" "No, thank God," said his companion, "for I never was upset in one." "What!" replied Mytton—"*never* upset in a gig? What a d—d slow fellow you must have been all your life;" and, running his near wheel up the bank, over they both went, fortunately without either being much injured!

Shortly after Mr. Mytton attained his majority, he

gave a horse-dealer, named Clarke, of Meole, in Shropshire, an order to purchase for him some carriage horses. Putting one of them into a gig, *tandem*, to see, as he expressed himself, " whether he would make a good leader," he asked the dealer, who sat beside him, *if he thought he was a good timber-jumper?* On the dealer expressing a doubt, Mytton exclaimed, " Then we'll try him "; and a closed turnpike-gate (at Hanwood) being before him, he gave the horse his head, and a flanker with his whip at the same moment, when he cleared the gate in beautiful style, leaving Mytton and the dealer, and the other horse, all on the nether side of the gate; and fortunately all alive, although the gig was much injured. He once had a horse that would rear up in his gig, at the word of command, until the hinder part of it absolutely touched the ground; and, although he was much given to display this dangerous accomplishment, no accident was the result.

I was myself once passing through the town of Oswestry, only two hours too late to have witnessed a most singular performance of a team of coach horses of his, which he had been exercising in a break. Finding they had gotten the better of him, he contrived to quit the carriage without injury, and the

Drawn and Etched by H. Aiken and T. J. Rawlins

"I wonder whether he is a good timber jumper!"

horses being at liberty, ran at full speed into the town of Oswestry. Unfortunately a gateway presented itself, into which they dashed, and now for the finish. The said gateway led into a parallel street, but, narrowing as it lengthened, there was, towards the further end of it, room for the horses but not for the carriage to pass. The consequence was, the four horses, breaking all their harness by the shock, tumbled head over heels into the street, and strange to say, not one of them was killed. So much for his exploits in harness.

Perhaps the most awful accident that ever happened to this most extraordinary man, was on his return, after dark, from a race-course, in his travelling carriage and four. The postboys mistook an old road, which had been stopped up, for the right one; and entered it, *down hill too*, at the rate of fourteen miles in the hour, when they came suddenly in contact with some fallen trees, which were placed across it as a barrier. The force of the shock may be imagined; the carriage was broken to pieces; the servant was pitched from his seat to a very considerable distance, sustaining a fracture of the skull from the fall; and Mytton was a good deal hurt—any other man, perhaps, would have been killed, as he was fast asleep at the time. The fate of the horses and the boys I do not at this moment recollect; but the servant—who by good conduct was promoted by degrees to the post of valet de chambre to Mr. M. from being a boy in my stable—has, I fear, never recovered from the effects of this dire mishap.

But Mr. Mytton appeared, at least wished to be supposed to be, indifferent to pain. A very few days after he had had so bad a fall with his own hounds as to occasion the dislocation of three ribs, and was otherwise much bruised, a friend in Wales, unconscious of his accident, sent him a fox in a bag, with a hint that, if turned out on the morrow, he would be sure to afford sport, as *he was only just caught*. "To-morrow, then," said Mytton, "will we run him"; and although he was lifted upon his horse, having his body swathed with rollers, and also writhing with pain, he took the lead of all the field, upon a horse he called "The Devil," and was never headed by any man, till he killed his fox, at the end of a capital hour's run. He was very near fainting from the severity of this trial; but I remember his telling me, *he would not have been seen to faint, for ten thousand pounds.*

Upon another somewhat similar occasion, he showed

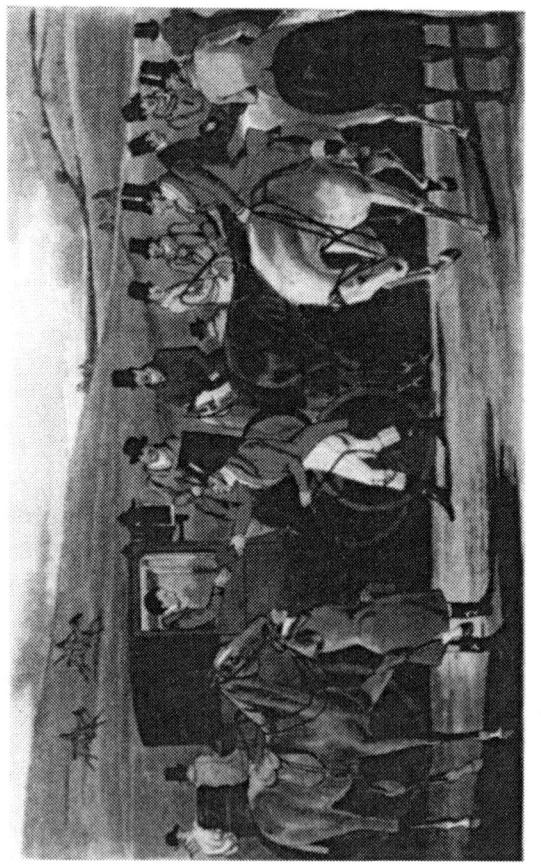

Drawn & Etched by H. Alken

The "Meet," with Lord Derby's Stag-hounds.

his disregard of pain. He was on his return from the field, with two of his ribs displaced, and evidently suffering much from a fall. To enable him to cut off an angle, he got into a fold-yard, but could not get out of it unless by riding over some high rails, which he did, in that state.

In the hilarity of high animal spirits he performed some feats that were ludicrous, and others that were painful to witness. Amongst the former was his appearance with Lord Derby's stag-hounds, when he was taken for a London tailor. Happening to be in town in the hunting season, he had a desire to see those celebrated hounds, and Tilbury sent out a horse for the purpose. On his arrival at the place of meeting in a cab, which he had driven at an awful rate, he attracted the notice of the throng, to all of whom, save one, he was a stranger. "What a buck he is!" said one. "Who the d—l is he?" said another. "*He is a tailor from London,*" said several, all of which remarks were carefully re-echoed to him by his friend. Mytton said nothing, but the tables were soon turned when Lord Derby's carriage drove up. "What, MYTTON!" exclaimed Lord Stanley,[1] "who would have thought of seeing *you* here"—putting out his

[1] Now Earl of Derby.

hand to welcome him. "Why, to tell you the truth, Stanley," said Mytton, "I have ridden over many a good fellow in my own country, but I never rode over a Cockney, and I am come here to-day for that sole purpose."

His treatment of a London Jew money-lender was not amiss. Being wearied by delay, he hired two coal-heavers to knock at his door every second hour throughout the night, until the money was forthcoming. But this anecdote furnishes a painful recollection on the subject of money-lending. A few years back he borrowed ten thousand pounds on an annuity at high interest, and lent nine of it to a friend who has never been seen in Europe since! This, although a type of the man, is no matter for joking; but the following may be looked upon as frolics. He had a parson and a doctor dining with him one evening at Halston, and at a certain hour of the night they mounted their horses to return to their homes. Having a carter's frock, and a brace of pistols loaded with blank cartridges, at hand, Mytton mounted a hack, and by a circuitous route headed and met them on the road, when letting fly both barrels at them, and calling to them to "stand and deliver," he declared they never rode half so fast in their lives as they did from that

Drawn and Etched by H. Alken

"Stand and deliver."

Drawn and Etched by H. Aiken

A new Hunter — Tallyho! Tallyho!

place to Oswestry, with himself at their heels. On another occasion he was told that the late George Underhill, the celebrated Shropshire horse-dealer, was in his house, on his road from Chester fair. Sending for him into his dining-room, he made him excessively drunk and put him to bed with two bull-dogs and a bear! He once rode this bear into his drawing-room, in full hunting costume. The animal carried him very quietly for a certain time; but on being pricked by the spur he bit his rider through the calf of his leg, inflicting a severe wound. The mention of this bear reminds me of another amusing anecdote. Having sent one of his stable boys with a hack to meet a friend who was coming by a coach, the latter exclaimed, on riding into the Halston stable-yard, " Ah! *bruin!* "—alluding to the bear, " Oh yes, sir," observed the lad, " we always *brews* twice a week at Halston." What I am now going to relate I know not how to define, for in most people's opinion it rather exceeds a joke. As we were eating some supper one night in the coffee-room of the hotel at Chester, during the race week, a gentleman, who was a stranger to us all, was standing with his back to the fire, talking very loudly, having drunk too much wine. " I'll stop him," said Mytton; and getting behind him unperceived, put a red-hot coal into his pocket.

But I have a better, inasmuch as it was a more harmless, joke, to relate with respect to George Underhill, the horse-dealer. He rode over one day to Halston, to dun Mr. Mytton for his demand upon him, which, I believe, was rather a large one. After having been made comfortable in the steward's room, Mytton addressed him thus: "Well, George, here (handing him a letter) is an order for *all* your money. Call on this gentleman, as you pass through Shrewsbury, and he will give it to you *in full.*" Now this gentleman—also a banker—was one of the governors of the Lunatic Asylum, and the order for payment ran thus:

Halston.

Sir,

Admit the bearer, George Underhill, into the Lunatic Asylum.

Your obedient servant,

John Mytton.

The mention of the trick he paid the Jew money-lender bears a resemblance to one he paid a toll-keeper near his own house, who had demanded and received double toll from him on the score of its being past twelve o'clock at night, whereas it was only just eleven, and it had been once before paid during the day. Although it was a bitter cold night, Mytton waited till the toll-keeper was warm in his bed, and then repassed the gate, of course without paying toll. Nor did the frolic end here. No sooner was the fellow once more in bed, than the word "Gate" again resounded in his ears; and finding out whom he had to deal with, he gladly returned the money, and enjoyed the rest of the night in repose.

The history of this bear may not be unworthy of notice. Mytton purchased her (it was a female bear) when very young, together with a monkey, from a strolling showman who was passing through Ellesmere, a town five miles distant from Halston, for the sum of thirty-five pounds for the two. Having been upwards of seven years in his possession and handled at an early age, the former was tolerably tracticable for an animal so naturally savage; but she was not to be trifled with by strangers. It was indeed in consequence of her injuring one of the servants of the establishment that Mytton ordered her to be put to death, which, as fire-arms were not resorted to, was said to have been a very difficult undertaking. In self-defence she severely wounded one of her assailants.

The death of the monkey was quite in character

with his life—bordering strongly on the ludicrous. Like his master, Jacko was fond of his bottle, and mistaking a jar of Day and Martin's blacking for something of a more vinuous quality, he drank so freely of it as to produce an illness which deprived him of his eye-sight, and eventually caused his death. Many of his exploits have been related to me, such as his performance, after hounds, on the horse called The Devil, but as I have no personal knowledge of them, I am unwilling to give them publicity. They bear too close a resemblance to some old Joe Miller stories of the same amusing animal.

It is said of Napoleon, that he wished to banish the word "*impossible*" from the French Dictionary. Mytton must have had some such desire; for he once told me, at Halston, that he had a filly in his racing stable which should win the Oaks (she was named in those stakes), and afterwards *she herself should put them into his pocket.* On my ridiculing the idea, he said—"Why not? She will now put both her hind feet into my pockets, and why not her mouth?" I accompanied him to the stable, and to my horror witnessed the latter exhibition. Mytton laid himself down at full length under her belly, with his bare head between her heels, and first taking up one foot

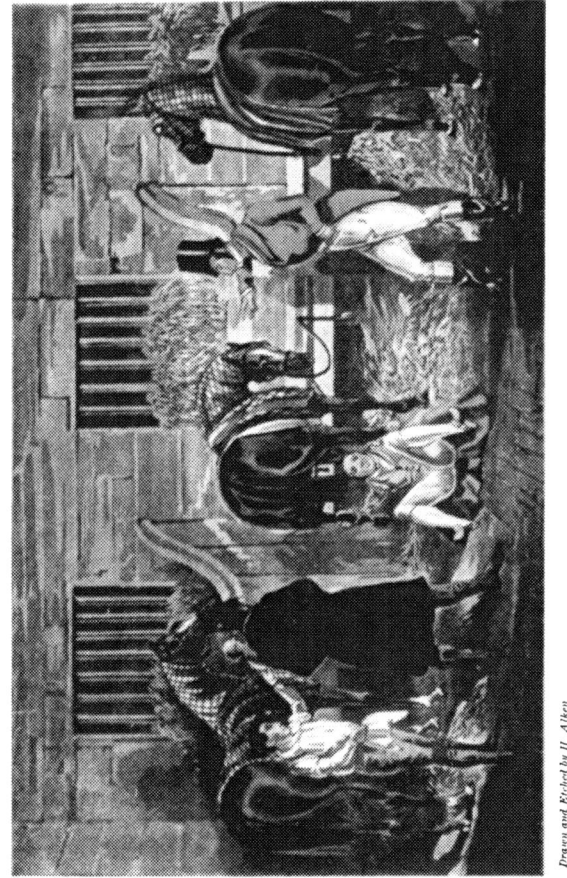

Drawn and Etched by H. Alken

The Oaks filly.

and then the other, placed them both in the pockets of his dressing gown. William Dilly, his trainer, witnessed all this as well as myself; but on his attempting to take liberties with a horse called Oswestry, in the next box, who was of a very different temper, his worthy servant thus addressed him. "You will do that once too often, sir, with *this* horse; and, good-tempered as she is, should your Oaks filly become alarmed, she will surely knock out your brains." "Good advice, Mr. Dilly," said I, as I turned away from the awful scene; "but you may spare your breath; John Mytton will be John Mytton; he heareth not the voice of the charmer, charm he never so wisely, and, like Homer's divinities, is always in mischief."

But I must not do, as Homer did by his heroes, make mine a savage. And yet how are we to define some of the darings and doings of this extraordinary man! For example, the following description of an evening at Halston is given by me in the Sporting Magazine just ten years back, and, strange enough, to a very day from the present writing. After describing a display of young foxes which were brought into the dinner-room for inspection, I thus proceed: — "We were now offered the company of the *bear*, but to a man declined the honour. By way of a finish, however, we had one turn-up between a Spanish bull-dog and an animal called *Blood* — a cross between a Spanish bull-dog and an English mastiff; when our host, thinking that Blood was getting *bloody*, and might kill the other dog, ran at him and pinned him by the nose; and although weighing more than seventy pounds, he raised him from the ground with his teeth, holding him suspended for at least a minute, without the smallest assistance from his hands." Neither is this a solitary instance of his contest with ferocious dogs. Returning from hunting one day, he, with some others, called to lunch at a farm-house called the Berries, near Whitchurch, where there was a very large and savage dog chained in the yard. "Pray don't go near him, Mr. Mytton," said his owner, "for he will tear you in pieces if you do." This was enough for Mytton; so pulling a silk handkerchief out of the pocket of a friend, and lapping it around his left hand, he advanced with it extended towards the dog, who immediately seized it with his mouth. Reader—I fancy I see you shudder! But don't be alarmed; and when you hear the sequel perhaps you will think that the dog might have been the greater sufferer of the two, provided blood had been drawn. Catching him by the back of the neck, however, with

LIFE OF MYTTON

his right hand, Mytton instantly pinned the animal by the nose with his teeth; and getting the other hand at liberty, so pummelled his opponent that he had scarcely any life left in him. As might be expected, the dog never afterwards liked the look of his brother bull-dog or even a red coat, but slunk into his kennel on the approach of either one or the other.

The terms good-natured and good-tempered are very often confounded by being indiscriminately applied to the same person or animal, whereas they admit of no inconsiderable distinction; and we have a striking instance here. Mytton, by nature, was kind and beneficent to a degree very rarely witnessed. I will not go so far as to say—what Crabbe's son says of him—that "no sympathy was like his," yet, with a pretended insensibility to the common sympathies of our nature, he never saw misery that he did not wish to relieve it. The conflicting elements of his character, or, more properly speaking, some parts of his conduct, may appear to give the lie to this; yet all who knew the man know that I have spoken the truth, and the tears of the multitude that were shed at his grave place it beyond dispute. In his temper he was sudden and violent, and, like Achilles, impatient of restraint; yet his wrath endured but the twinkling of an eye, and in forgiveness of injuries he had no equal within my knowledge of mankind. What a paradox then is here! With all his native goodness of heart, he appeared to wish to make the world believe he cared no more than Dionysius for the gods what the world thought or said of him; and, although his good sense must have convinced him that there is a profligacy of spirit in defying the rules of decorum, he oftentimes acted as if he considered every law, human or divine, of little worth. But, I say again—what a paradox is here! The man who had no "*regard* to his good name," has left a good name behind him that will be remembered and cherished in Shropshire for many, many, years to come—and for deeds that would have done honour to an apostle. When I say that he was charitable to the poor, and gave them two bushels of wheat a week the year round, I give him credit for little more than might be expected from a man of his means, and of a nature generous to prodigality; but I have reason to believe no one knew half the extent of his beneficent acts. 'Tis said of charity, that it admits of no error but excess; and to excess did he often carry it, as I shall presently have occasion to show. In fact, he was as extravagant in his virtues as in his vices—or, I would rather say, in his failings. The perfection of man's moral nature is said to be forgiveness of injuries, but Mytton went a point beyond this. Even that hard injunction of the gospel, *to love an enemy*—the characteristic of a religion not of man but of God, and, as the author of the Adventurer observes, "could have been delivered as a precept only," for society could not exist under its practice—was no paradox with him, as I shall produce several instances to prove.

But to return to his nature. Pythagoras being asked in what man could resemble the Divinity, replied — "in beneficence and truth." Here again we have a paradox. The man who sometimes assumed the character of a fiend, and appeared to strive against the native goodness of his heart, answers to that of the Deity; for inasmuch as his beneficence was unquestionable, so was his veracity unimpeachable. Setting aside jesting, in which none dealt more largely,—in fact, he was a sort of human Silenus, — no man could with more safety be spoken after than Mytton could. I am quite certain nothing could have induced him to have uttered a premeditated untruth, for any unworthy purpose! and there was a good-humoured and affectionate simplicity about him that rendered him a great favourite in his neighbourhood. Again—he was no backbiter. On the contrary, when he heard the "voice of slander rankle on the ear," he always turned the discourse—saying as my Uncle Toby did, when his Corporal was reckoning up all the rascals of his regiment, "we will speak of this another time." In his dealings with the world he was a man of strict honour and probity; and without justifying his extravagance, I may be allowed to say that his chief concern, after the last estates he could sell were disposed of, was not whether he himself might be left destitute, but whether there would be enough to pay his creditors *in full*. As a master he was kindest of the kind, and a liberal and most considerate landlord. Surely then this man must have been either counterfeiting a nature not his own,[1] or he must have been, to a certain extent and on certain points, a madman! No doubt, he did the one; and no doubt he was the other!

The worst feature in poor Mytton's disposition, and what may be termed the reigning error of his life was,

[1] The following was related to me by the medical gentleman, at Oswestry (now living), who attended the accouchement of the *first* Mrs. Mytton. "Mr. Mytton," said he, "was in the billiard room, when I went to inform him of the birth. *What is it?* he inquired. On my telling him it was a girl, he swore he would have it smothered—but, throwing himself on a sofa, gave vent to his feelings in a flood of tears, and his anxiety for the well-doing of his lady would have done honour to any man."

not only that he would not bow to reproof, much less kiss the rod, but he would suffer no man either to counsel or advise him. There was, however, none of "*obsequium amicos, veritas odium, parit,*" that Terence speaks of, about him, for he always received it in good part, being neither flattered nor offended ; but he would not take advice even when given to him by his sincerest friends, and with the purest and most disinterested motives. He always considered it an impeachment of his understanding, generally exclaiming to those who offered it— " What the d—l is the use of my having a head on my own shoulders, if I am obliged to make use of yours?" But, unfortunately, at times his ears were deaf to the voice of *reason*, as the following anecdote will show :—Previously to the disposal of the first property that he sold, I happened to be at Halston, and was about to accompany him to Lichfield races, where each had horses to run. Just before we set out, his agent, the late Mr. Longueville, of Oswestry, arrived at the house and wished to speak to me. As nearly as I can recollect, the following were his exact words :— " I have reason to believe you can say as much to Mr. Mytton as any man can ; will you have the goodness to tell him you heard me say, that if he will be content to live on £6,000 per annum, for the next six years, he need not sell the fine old

Shrewsbury estate, that has been so many years in his family, and at the end of that period he shall not owe a guinea to any man." I fancy I see the form and features of my old friend, with the manner in which he received and replied to the flattering proposition, and many others who knew him as well as I did, will also have the picture in their mind's eye. Lolling back in his carriage, which was going at its usual pace, and picking a hole in his chin, as he was always wont to do when any thing particularly occupied his thoughts, he uttered not a syllable for the space of some minutes; when, suddenly changing his position, as if rousing from a deep reverie, he exclaimed, with vehemence—"You may tell Longueville to keep his advice to himself, *for I would not give a d—n to live on six thousand a year.*" Knowing his regard and esteem for that worthy gentleman, it was in vain to urge the subject any further, for there was that in his manner which convinced me he was not to be persuaded on this point by any man,—no, not though one rose from the dead. Hence is his ruin dated.

From the serious to the jocular is but a step; and the mention of this circumstance leads to a joke. A near relation was endeavouring to dissuade him from parting with a certain estate, on the score of its having been so long in the family. "How long?" inquired Mytton. "Above five hundred years," was the reply. "The devil it has!" resumed this most extraordinary man; "*then it is high time it should go out of it.*"

With a perfect contempt for the splendour of cold-hearted opulence, Mr. Mytton lived very much like a gentleman at Halston, where every thing was in keeping with his fortune and station in life. There was no unnecessary display—two men servants out of livery, and two in livery, being the full complement at the dinner table, nor did he indulge in the luxury of a man cook. Although himself a perfect stranger to the science of economy, his establishment was managed with considerable regularity; and notwithstanding the consumption of good things in the servants' hall, for the number of stable servants was great, it was not Halston that ruined him. It was that "largeness of heart, even as the sand that is on the sea shore," which Solomon possessed, but unaccompanied by his means as well as by his wisdom, which ruined Mr. Mytton; added to a lofty pride which disdained the littleness of prudence, and a sort of destroying spirit that appeared to run amuck at fortune. By a rough computation, and a knowledge of the property he sold, I should set down the sum total expended, at very little less than half a million sterling within the last fifteen years ! !

But how would this expenditure be accounted for if something like a schedule of his disbursements were to be called for? The task would be an Herculean one, but Horace would furnish a commentary upon it. Some persons hunt, says he; some race, some drink, some do one thing and some another; but Mytton, in sporting language, was "at all in the ring." His fox-hounds were kept by himself without any subscription, and upon a very extensive scale, with the additional expenses attending hunting two countries. His racing establishment was on a still larger scale, having often had from fifteen to twenty horses in training at the same time, and seldom less than eight. His average number, indeed, of thorough-bred stock at home and from home, including brood mares and young things, was about thirty-six! His game-preserves were likewise a most severe tax upon his income. Will it be credited that he paid one bill of £1,500 to a London game dealer, for pheasants and foxes alone! The formation of three miles of plantation which this game went, in part, to stock, must have cost him an immense sum; having had, for several years, as many as fifty able-bodied labourers in his employ

There is this line somewhere, though I cannot recollect where:

"Dress drains our cellars dry;"

but such was not the case at Halston, and I believe the satire applies to the ladies. It was hard to say, however, which was the better stocked of the two —Mr. Mytton's wardrobe or the Halston cellars. I once counted a hundred and fifty-two pairs of breeches and trousers, with a proportionate accompaniment of coats, waistcoats, &c., in the former; and I think I, on another occasion, described the "hogsheads of ale, standing like soldiers in close column, and wine enough in wood and bottle for a Roman Emperor," in the latter. The *clothes* he would put on his person, just as they came to his hand, or as his wild fancy prompted him, and I have seen him nearly destroy a new coat at once wearing. His shoes and boots, all London make, and very light, were also destroyed in an equally summary manner, in his long walks over the country, through or over every thing that came in his way. It is impossible even to guess at his annual expense in post-horses; but every post-boy in England lamented the fall of "Squire Mytton," their very best customer. I have reason to believe that the money he has at various times lost (not at play, for there I should say he was borne harmless[1]) would have purchased a pretty estate. I am afraid to say what was supposed to have been the amount of bank notes that were one night blown out of his carriage on his road from Doncaster races, but I have reason to believe it was several thousand pounds! His account of the affair was this :—He had been counting a large quantity of bank notes on the seat of his carriage—in which he was alone—with all the windows down; and falling asleep, did not awake until the night was far spent—his servant paying the charges on the road. An equinoctial gale having sprung up, carried great part of the notes away on its wings, verifying the proverb of "light come light go." It was always his custom to have a large sum of money in his travelling writing desk, but it was more than usually large at this time, in consequence of his having broken the banks of two well known London Hells on the eve of his departure from London for Doncaster. Like Democritus, however, Mytton laughed at every thing, and always spoke of this as a very good joke. I have seen him, when he has been going a journey, take a lot of bank notes out of his desk, and rolling them into

---

[1] He was a very dangerous man with a dice-box in his hand. Wine gave him courage, which generally tells at hazard.

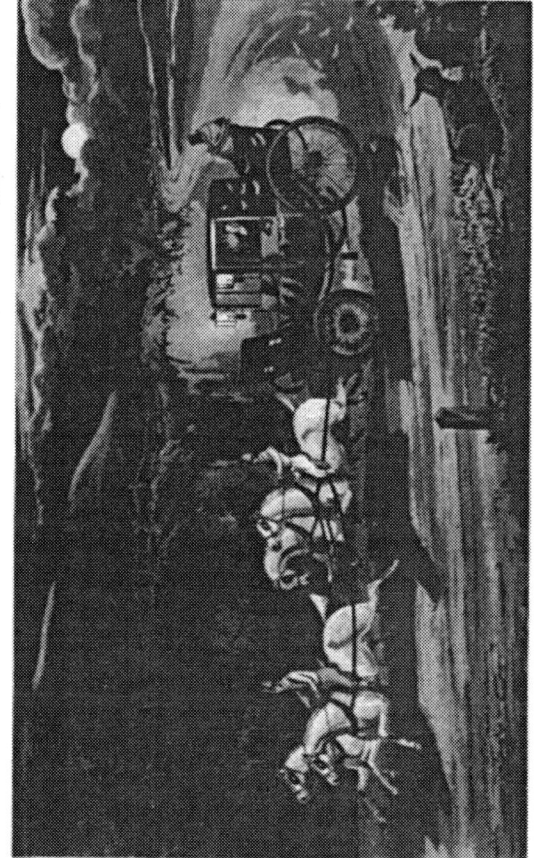

"Light come, light go".

Drawn and Etched by H. Aiken

a lump, throw them at his servant's head, as if they had been waste paper; but his chaplain used to say, he always knew what the lump contained, and how far it would carry him—a fact by no means so clear to me. I picked up one of these lumps some years since in the plantations at Halston containing £37, which had been there some days by its appearance; and as he never had pockets in his breeches, such occurrences must have been frequent.

Perhaps there was one *cause* of expense incurred by John Mytton that is not to be traced to any other man; but, as Charles the Fifth profanely boasted that "there was only one God and one Charles," surely there never was but one John Mytton. This said John Mytton would never open letters secured by wafers, unless he were acquainted with the hand-writing. Thus were tradesmen's applications unanswered till their patience became exhausted and law proceedings were in consequence resorted to. But he cared no more for writs than he did for any thing else, as they, of course, were sent to his solicitor, and all he knew of them, in his prosperity, was, that he paid for them. So popular, however, was he with the lower orders, that, in his prosperous days, I do not think a bailiff in the four surrounding counties would have arrested him, had he been instructed so to do.

It is impossible to separate the sort of *vis comica* that attached itself to the various acts of imprudence of my, otherwise, truly nobly-minded friend; and perhaps the anecdote of the London game-dealer, and his £1,500 bill, is about as amusing as any. On his arrival at Halston, he presented it himself to his debtor; but it appeared from his subsequent conduct that he little thought it would have been paid, *without something like a scrutiny into its merits*. Here, however, was John Mytton, "*sui generis*," again. "Give me a pen and ink," said he, casting his eye over the amount: and, scratching the words, "*Right*, John Mytton," with his usual expedition, under it, exclaimed, "there, take it to my agent, and get the money." As may be supposed, the joy of this man was excessive, but its out-break was reserved until he saw the agent at Oswestry draw a cheque at sight for the entire sum. It was then no longer to be restrained, and thus did the dealer in dogs, foxes, pheasants, and monkeys, *et hoc genus omne*, give vent to the noble feelings of his nature. "Oh, my dear sir," said he, "what can I do for *you*, in return for all this kindness?" "I have done you no kindness," said the agent; "the only favour you can confer upon me is, never to let me see or hear of you again." This however did not satisfy the pheasant-merchant, who was anxious, if not to make a display of his gratitude, at all events to propitiate the good will of the agent, and once more addressed him. "Pray, sir," said he, "are you a married gentleman?" On being answered in the affirmative, the nature of the donation was determined upon. "Then, sir," added he, "*allow me to present your lady with a monkey!*" Well might the man of law have exclaimed—

"Quicquid id est timeo Danaos et dona ferentes;"

but when he was made acquainted with the nature of the gift, the would-be giver was very soon despatched, and I never heard whether he again made his appearance, on a similar errand, at Halston.

The next anecdote that presents itself to my mind arose out of my seeing him get out of his carriage at a cover's side and walk towards his hunter, to mount him. "*There he goes,*" said Tom Penn; "*he's a lily ain't he.* Give him two hundred thousand a year, and I'll bet a hundred he's in debt in foive (five) years." But it is necessary to say who this Tom Penn is, or rather *was*, for he is also in his grave, having broken his neck in hunting. He was pad-groom to Sir Watkin

Williams Wynn, Bart., much looked up to, and consequently often consulted, for his correct judgment of a hunter, by the help of which, although an excellent servant, he was one of the most impudent fellows that ever wore a livery—or perhaps more properly speaking, what is known in the lower world as "a regular cool hand."

Now a question arises, not unworthy of discussion. Did the late Mr. Mytton really enjoy life amidst all this profusion of expenditure; and was he, in the best of his days, in a situation that many poor men would covet? This, I think, admits of a doubt. It is true he had most of the requisites for a man of a noble fortune that Horace granted to his friend Tibullus; but one thing was wanting — the "*artemque fruendi*"—*the art of enjoying it*, to which he, Mytton, was a stranger. Indeed, to a vitiated palate, always calling for fresh gratifications, the wealth of Crœsus might fail in procuring that one thing wanting; but there was something about my friend that gave one the idea that, to him it was peculiarly denied. There was that about him which resembled the restlessness of the hyena; and whether in the pursuit of his pastimes, or the gratification of his passions, there was an unsteadiness throughout which evidently showed, that, beyond the excitement of the passing moment, nothing afforded him sterling pleasure. All those who watched his actions might perceive, that his object was to have a taste of every thing that was alluring and delicious; and, like the bee, to rove from flower to flower, merely culling a little of the sweets of each. Look, for example, at the various sources of amusement Halston afforded, and the small share of calm enjoyment they appeared to afford the owner of them. What elegant dinners have I seen him sit down to at his own table, with no more appetite to partake of them, than an alderman has when singing "*Non nobis, Domine*"—having an hour or two before been eating fat bacon and drinking strong ale at some tenant's or other farm house on his road home from his field pursuits. Again—if he had a good race-horse in his stables he would run him off his legs, nearly to his destruction; and he served his favourite hunters in the same manner. All this could have been reconciled with youthful enthusiasm, and Welch blood; but with Mytton it could be only traced to one cause, which grew with his growth, but did not quit him in his manhood, and finally plunged him into the abyss of misery!

But if the proprietor of it himself was not satisfied with the resources which Halston afforded, few of his friends were so unreasonable as to have looked for amusement and not found it, for indeed the very proprietor of it alone, with his various appendants and his frolics, was a constant source of mirth. A celebrated historian of the Augustan age, however, now presents himself to my view, and wisely reminds me, that decency is a principal virtue in an historian, and that he should preserve the characters of the persons as well as the dignity of the actions of those of which he treats. Heretofore I trust I have written nothing that can be construed into more than an allowable levity of style, inseparable from the chronicling of the sayings and doings of such a character as is before me ; and as one object is to display it in every variety of colour—and the rainbow itself has not more—I must here introduce a description of an evening at Halston from my own pen, published ten years since in the Sporting Magazine. As it commences with an apology I shall offer none here.

"'What Cato did, and Addison approved, cannot be wrong,' said a learned and accomplished gentleman of the last century, when he put a period to a miserable existence. Now as the great essayist here named introduced his friend, Sir Roger's chaplain, to the world, perhaps I may be allowed to introduce

Mr. Mytton's. He is a very old acquaintance of mine, and I know he will pardon me for doing so. I cannot exactly say he is to his patron what Mæcenas was to Augustus, or what Falstaff was to Henry; but rather what Crispus was to the Roman Emperors. He (Crispus) lived with four of them; joked with all of them; and quarrelled with none of them—though their ears were perhaps more tender than their hearts. The Halston Chaplain, however, is entitled to a place in the *Sporting Magazine*, having given birth to as much sport as ever was seen in a race, a cock-pit, or a fox-chase. In a style peculiarly his own, he says more good things than any other man I ever met with, and by his good humour, and inoffensive jokes, has often made the old Halston welkin ring.

"The connection between them commenced thus :—Soon after the Chaplain left the University, he resided in the neighbourhood of Halston, and was fixed upon as a sort of friendly preceptor to the heir apparent to the estate, both before, and after, he left Westminster School; and here, perhaps, one of the best anecdotes has its source. It appears there was some difficulty in persuading the young Squire to go to College; and when we consider a little, our wonder ceases. October is the best month for pheasant-shooting; Christmas lasts till Easter at Halston; and hunting, fishing, and shooting, last all the year round. The Chaplain, however, was employed to use all his eloquence to induce him to go, and the following dialogue passed between them:

"*Chaplain.* My good sir, you must go to Oxford: you must, indeed, sir!

"*Mr. Mytton.* I'll see you ——— first.

"*Chaplain.* Upon my word, sir, you must go. Every man of fortune ought to go to Christ Church, if only for a term or so.

"*Mr. Mytton.* Well, then, if I do go, I will go on the following terms.

"*Chaplain.* What are they, sir?

"*Mr. Mytton.* Why—that I never open a book.

"*Chaplain.* Not the least occasion—not the smallest I assure you.

"*Mr. Mytton.* Very well then, I don't mind going,

provided I read nothing but the Racing Calendar, and the Stud Book.

"*Chaplain.* Excellent books, sir; they will do very well indeed.

"The next amusing anecdote of the Chaplain arose out of the following circumstance:—Going one morning, as usual, to serve the family church at Halston, Mr. Mytton contrived to take his sermon out of his pocket, and substitute in its place the last number of the *Sporting Magazine.* When the Chaplain had mounted the rostrum, and was preparing to throw off, he found his mistake, and, of course, had nothing to do but to apologise to his hearers for the loss of his sermon, and, 'with a well-bred whisper, close the scene.' It is also said of him, that having a tender regard for his patron, and knowing the natural kindness of his disposition, he has always avoided wantonly hurting his feelings; so that, on some occasions, when it has been his intention to preach a sermon, which, to use his own words, he feared might 'hit him hard,' he has been prepared with another, 'in case the Squire should be in church.'

"There is another story of the Chaplain, which,

though it has been before recorded in the *Sporting Magazine*, yet it was not placed to his credit, but to him alone is it due. About five years back, he applied to his Diocesan to give him a living, and the Bishop promised him the first that was vacant. Having a pretty private fortune of his own, and not aspiring to a mitre, the Chaplain took the liberty of requesting that his Lordship would not send him into the Welch mountains, but give him an English living. The Bishop, knowing him to be a thorough-bred Welchman (and, indeed, no one could take him for a half-bred one), demanded him his reasons for such a request? 'Why, my Lord,' said the Chaplain, 'my wife does not speak Welch.'— 'Your wife, sir!' said his Diocesan, 'what has your wife to do with it? She does not preach, does she!'—'No, my Lord,' said the Chaplain, '*but she lectures!*' The Bishop, as may be expected, took all this in good part, and the Chaplain was soon afterwards exalted to a living in the wildest part of the Welch mountains.

"No man was ever more free from guile than the Chaplain of Halston, and Rector of ———. Indeed, some of his intimate friends have doubted whether he has enough of this subtle art to enable him to go through the world with *éclat*. Being once on a visit at an old lady's house, who prided herself on the excellence of her cook, he was requested to carve the bottom dish. On being asked to help the old lady herself, he addressed her thus:—'Pray, madam, how do you like it? *Here is some very much done,—some very little done,—and some not done at all.*' On another occasion he was dining with an old gentleman in Gloucestershire, who plumed himself on the celebrity of his ale. On hearing that the chaplain was a Welchman, and reckoned a good judge, he ordered a fresh cask to be tapped, and pledged him in a bumper of it after his cheese. No encomium being passed on it, the old gentleman ventured to ask him how he liked his ale?—'Why, sir,' said the chaplain, '*we should call it very good small beer in Wales.*'

"I have before observed, that the Halston chaplain can neither be compared to Mæcenas, nor to Falstaff—being completely '*sui generis.*' Some years since, however, he put me in mind of a scene between the latter and his prince. We had had rather a hard night at Halston, and our host was taking a nap, at full length, on the sofa. After looking at him for some time, his old preceptor broke out into the following soliloquy: ' Only think, sir, what the Squire, with his abilities, *might have been*, and only see what *he is !* '

"On Sunday last, as is his usual custom after the duties of the morning, the chaplain entered upon those of the evening, and took his place behind the beef. Here, Lord Chesterfield himself never displayed a better grace; for amid the blaze and radiance of nine gold and three silver cups—the fruits of some well-contested races—his rosy face outshone them all; and it may be said of him, without offence to any one, that he is equally orthodox in the bottle as in the wood—being a Christian at all times, and one of the best-natured parsons in the universe."

Alas! the chaplain did not long survive his friend and patron; and it is generally believed, that his accumulated distresses, his fallen state, and his miserable end, accelerated his own death. At all events, I am informed that the words "poor Mytton" were nearly the last he uttered.

PART II

WITH what extraordinary characters of ancient and modern times would John Mytton stand a comparison? With Nero? Yes; for Nero fiddled whilst Rome was burning, and Mytton would have laughed had he seen Halston in flames. But Nero murdered his mother, and Mytton made a noble provision for his.[1] With Timon of Athens? Yes, as a spendthrift; but the one hated, and the other was kind to, all mankind. With Napoleon Bonaparte? Yes, for his historian says of him—"Extreme agitation was the basis of his existence; motion was his repose; he lived in a hurricane, and fattened on anxiety and care." But one drank coffee seven times a day, and the other drank as many bottles of port wine!! With the poet Byron? Yes, inasmuch as each was at Harrow school, and each fought eight pitched battles during the time he remained there. With Savage — immortalized by his biographer, Johnson? Yes, as far as each had a distinctive mark of genius and originality, which ranks

---
[1] He added £500 per annum to her jointure.

high amongst the qualities of the human mind, and each was very deficient in the τὸ πρέπον. But one was chiefly known by his poverty, his misfortunes, and his wit; the other inherited riches, and might have set fortune's malice at defiance.

The strongest resemblance I can select, is between the characters of the celebrated Earl of Rochester and the subject of this memoir; although in the points on which they differ, the balance is favourable to the latter. Let us select the most prominent features and see how far they tally, and in what they differ:—

Rochester's person was well shaped, and no man showed more good breeding, in society. Ditto John Mytton.

Rochester thought his constitution was so strong, that nothing could hurt it. Ditto John Mytton.

"Rochester," says Bishop Burnet, "had a violent love of pleasure, and a disposition to extravagant mirth; the one involved him in great sensuality; the other led him to many odd adventures and frolics, in which he was often in hazard of his life." Ditto John Mytton.

LIFE OF MYTTON

Rochester was turned loose into the world at a very early age, and so was John Mytton. The one entered the navy, the other the Seventh Hussars.

Rochester distinguished himself in an engagement. Mytton was never in one.

Rochester once made himself a mountebank. Mytton was always more or less one.

Rochester was drunk for five years continually. Mytton beat him by seven.[1]

Rochester "pursued low amours, in mean disguises." Mytton, in *propriâ personâ*, seldom pursued any other.

Rochester slunk away from his friend in a street-row. Mytton rather would have remained to have been pummelled to death.

The Duke of Buckingham left it on record that

---

[1] I am sorry to say one of his oldest friends, and a regular "pot-companion," made an affidavit—to serve a certain purpose—that he (Mytton) had been drunk for twelve successive years! I think it would have been better that he had had recourse to the "*Non mi recordo.*"

Rochester refused to fight him. Mytton was never put to that test.

Rochester wrote libels, in which he did not stick to truth. Mytton never said illnatured things, much less published them.

Rochester was eminent for the vigour of his colloquial wit. Mytton was deaf, and therefore could not shine in conversation. He dealt, chiefly, in practical jokes.

Rochester is mentioned by Wood as the best scholar of all the nobility. Mytton might have harangued an Athenian mob, if he had gone steadily through Harrow, or Westminster school.

Burnet says, " Rochester played many wild frolics which it is not for his honour that we should remember." Ditto John Mytton.

Burnet " touched as tenderly as occasion would bear " Rochester's faults. Mytton's spiritual adviser never touched his at all, if he could avoid it.

The good Bishop tells us Dr. Balfour " drew

Rochester to read such books as were most likely to bring him back to love learning and study." Mytton's tutor recommended the Racing Calendar and the Stud Book; nevertheless he was well read in the classics, though perhaps not so well as Rochester was. The natural talent of each was excellent; each was generous and kind-hearted; and "*video meliora proboque; deteriora sequor,*" "I see what is better and approve it; but follow what is worse," would have been a suitable motto for both. But Rochester was profane, which Mytton never was.

But I must draw this parallel to a close. Rochester was charitable to the poor and kind to his servants, and so was Mytton—perhaps to a still greater degree.

Rochester made himself mad with drink.—Ditto John Mytton. Was not the best of husbands.—Ditto John Mytton. Trusted to a death-bed repentance.—Ditto John Mytton. Promised to amend his life if he recovered from his severe illness. So did old Nick—at least so the story goes; but John Mytton never promised what he did not *think* he should perform. The one exhausted his life at the age of thirty-three, and the other of thirty-eight; and although both entered the vineyard at nearly the eleventh hour—for sackcloth and ashes suited neither of their tastes—they both died in penitence and prayer.

Mr. Mytton's amours, like Jupiter's, are too numerous for recital, yet having been for the most part of the lowest description, they were chiefly injurious only to himself, and had nothing to do with the heart. But there was this peculiarity in them: — I am quite sure Mr. Mytton never attempted the wife of a friend—no, nor even his mistress! Each would have been as safe in his hands as the beautiful captive was in those of Scipio, or the wife and daughters of Darius in the tent of Alexander the Great. Indeed I never heard of his *laying siege* to the virtue of any woman, but if in the market, he was sure to be the best bidder; and I fear I must own, that he once or twice took it by storm. Some of his offers for capitulation, however, were truly ridiculous, though all in character with the man. For example—he once wrote a note to a certain celebrated singer, whom he had only seen for half an hour, at a musical festival, requesting the honour of an interview the next day, and enclosing a cheque at sight, on the Oswestry bank, for five hundred guineas! The lady—who all the world know would have been quite satisfied with a ten pound note—having luckily never heard either of John Mytton or the Oswestry bank, returned the note with its valuable contents. This reminds me of the following lines in a poem called "The Passions," a fair specimen of heterogeneous bathos :—

"Human appetites how strong,
When love exults on fancy's fairy plains,
Or hunger views the mutton at the fire!"

His popularity, independently of family associations, and recollection of ages long since gone by; the dashing personal character, and extreme and unaffected good humour of the late squire of Halston; together with his fox-hounds, his race-horses, his game, his wine, his ale, and many other things besides, rendered him extremely popular in Shropshire; and if he had but been possessed of a fair share of the τὸ πρέπον, so much esteemed by the ancients, and so expressive of that *exterior* propriety of conduct, in the common intercourse of life, which the world is very unwilling to dispense with, he might have represented the County of Salop in parliament as long as he liked to have done so; it being the general opinion, that almost all the independent freeholders would have supported him. But this is the class of all others who dislike seeing a gentleman sink in the social scale? and when I was last in Shropshire, I was sorry to find my old friend's popularity was on the wane. His honour and his honesty were still unsullied ; his heart was as kind as it ever had been ; but the nearly constant state of intoxication in which he lived, was, I could perceive, become somewhat insufferable to his oldest friends. Neither was this the worst. His associating himself with a late well-known sporting character, immeasurably inferior to himself in every possible point of view, gave the finishing blow, and who can wonder at it? for it must have been not only repulsive to good taste but extremely mortifying to his friends to see Mr. Mytton of Halston, with his natural talents and accomplishments, to say nothing of his connections, making a bosom friend of a man who had once filled the honourable post of a waterman to a hackney-coach stand ! But there are moral as well as fabulous Actæons in this world, who are surely devoured by objects of their own choosing, and here we have an instance of it. In what way however can we account for a mind that had tasted the learning and elegance of Athens and Rome finding itself at ease in such an unsuitable association ? Why only by its being reduced to a state of perfect apathy and imbecility by the repetition of vicious and debilitating indulgences.

There is but one excuse for a man being almost

perpetually intoxicated and prostituting the reason of the man to the appetite of the brute ; and that is—the attempt to divert grief which he has found it impossible to subdue. As a balm for wounds which can never heal, or under the accumulated pressure of pecuniary difficulties, the bottle will be resorted to so long as the world shall stand, and who can condemn the wretch that tries the experiment? But the subject of this memoir had not such excuses to plead for his excess in drinking, neither will I endeavour to find them for him. It was, however, to him the Circean cup—the bane of his respectability, his health, his happiness, and every thing that was dear to him as a man and a gentleman; and can this be marvelled at? It is written of Hercules, that he acquired his immense strength by feeding on the marrow of lions, and how powerful must have been the stimulus of the almost unheard-of quantity of from *four* to *six* bottles of port wine *daily*, on that volcanic excitability of mind, which was, not only by nature, Mr. Mytton's, but which had been acted upon, and increased, by a severe affection of the brain, at an early period of life ! Thus, then, although I offer no excuse for his drinking, his drinking—for men are tried by wine, says the proverb, as metals are by fire—furnishes excuses, I should rather have said apologies, for his conduct, inasmuch as his reason was, to a certain extent, lost in delirium, caused by the fumes of wine, on an already somewhat distempered brain. Many of his acts were not the acts of John Mytton but of a man *mad, half by nature, and half by wine,* and I think his best and dearest friends are decidedly of my opinion.

From this account of its Host, it may be supposed that Halston was a scene of general dissipation and riot. By no means. In short, I cannot bring to my recollection a single instance of being one of what may be termed a drunken party, during my frequent visits to the house. But this is accounted for in more ways than one. The host had always the start of his friends, in the first place; and in the next, long sittings were not in accordance with his restless disposition. In the summer he would jump out of the window, and be off. In the winter, he was anxious to get to the billiard table, which was always lighted up after coffee, for the amusement of himself and his friends, and here he was in his element. How then, it may be asked, did he consume that quantity of port wine? Why this question is easily answered. He shaved with a bottle of it on his toilet; he worked steadily at it throughout the day, by a glass or two at a time, and at least a bottle with his luncheon; and the after dinner and *after supper* work—not losing sight of it in the billiard room — completed the Herculean task. No wonder, then, that Alexander the Great has been called "a fool to him," in his Bacchanalian feats, at all events he would have been a good playfellow for him at Persepolis; or that —as Cicero said of Piso—"his breath smelt like a vintner's vault." He is, however, a memorable example of the comparatively harmless effects of *very good wine*, which he always had, and just of a proper age—about eight years old— for, assisted by exercise, such as he took, it was many years before it injured him. But alas— wine at length lost its charms. Brandy—which he was a stranger to when I was last at Halston—was substituted, and the constitution of John Mytton, *perhaps the hardest ever bestowed upon man*, was not proof against that.[1]

But away, for a moment, with all recollection of his ill-doings, and let us move onwards towards his good ones—for it is a loss to mankind when *good* actions are forgotten. Be assured, reader—whoever you may

[1] It would be absurd to offer apology for these remarks, after the inquest on the body of my departed friend, which went the round of the Newspapers. Besides my object being to rescue his memory from imputations that lie against it, and, in some cases *not unjustly*, it is in mercy —a dreadful alternative I admit—that I exhibit him to the world as both a drunkard and a madman.

be—that if all the kind, good, and charitable acts which poor drunken, mad, John Mytton performed, were placed in counterpoise to his bad ones, it would be more than *man* dared do to say which side might kick the beam. At all events, like charity, they would weigh heavily to his credit; and it is consoling to his friends to reflect, that although great part of that fine property he once possessed has passed away to others, and the too liberal possessor of it is in his grave, *those deeds still remain with him*. Man, it is true, is naturally a beneficent creature; but be the benefit he confers never so great, the manner of conferring it is the noblest part, and in allusion to my friend, let me illustrate this by one simple fact:—

When Mr. Mytton was at Calais, only a few months before his death, he chanced to be in a silversmith's shop, when a French soldier entered it, with a watch in his hand, which he said he wished to dispose of for the benefit of a sick comrade, who wanted some further comforts than a barrack afforded. On the silversmith objecting to the price demanded, Mr. Mytton threw down the money, and took up the watch. "Merciez,[1] Monsieur," said the soldier, and something else besides, expressive of his grateful feelings. "Take *this* to your

[1] Short for—*je vous remerciez*.

comrade *also,*" said Mytton, placing the watch in his hand. "Ah Monsieur Anglais!" exclaimed the man—"*Que vous dirai-je?*"[1]

Mytton replied, "RIEN."[2] Remember, reader! this was not in his golden days, when money was as dross; it was one of the last acts of a noble soul, performed out of almost the last of the wreck of a splendid income.

The sentimental Sterne would have made a pathetic story out of this little incident, whereas I shall leave it to speak for itself; but Mytton felt what Sterne only made others feel, neither does the difference between them rest here. The one is said to have whined over a dead ass, and starved a living mother. The other would have laughed at the dead donkey — perhaps have ridden him to death — but he settled a handsome annuity on his mother! Such instances, however, are of very ancient date; Aristides practised what Cato only preached.

Another instance of his excessive philanthropy and over-generous all-forgiving temper occurs to me at this moment, which I may here introduce, though

---
[1] What shall I say to you?   [2] *Nothing*.

perhaps not without somewhat retrograding in my arrangement.

As I was passing through Shrewsbury, some years back, on my road to Halston, I saw a servant of his in the town, and asked him if he had accompanied his master. "I have left Mr. Mytton's service, sir," said the man. "How so?" observed I, with surprise, knowing him to have been a favourite servant. His answer was, that in an evil hour he had been induced to alter a figure in a bill of Mr. Lucas, the Veterinary-surgeon, at Atherstone, who had attended one of his master's horses, and it having been discovered by the agent, he had been discharged. The morning after I arrived at Halston, I was told there was a person wanted to speak with me in the stable-yard, and there stood *John*, with a very sorrowful countenance. His object was to induce me to intercede for him with his master, and just as I was in the act of discussing the point, Mr. Mytton made his appearance. John protested it was the only instance of his dishonesty (and indeed the man bore an excellent character, having lived nine years previously with a clergyman in Shropshire); and that he should not have thought of committing it but for a certain ostler on the road, who persuaded him to it; and was about to proceed in the same suppli-

LIFE OF MYTTON

cating manner, when Mytton seized him by the collar, and giving him one of his horse-like kicks, told him to go into the servants' hall, and put on his livery again! John cared nothing for the kick; but on a very strong remonstrance from the agent—who indeed went so far as to say, he should throw up his agency if such conduct were passed over—John was once more drafted from Halston servants' hall.

I conceive no one knew the limits of Mr. Mytton's natural talents. No doubt they were excellent; and if instead of having been prostrated to the excess of wine, and its concomitant dissipation, they had been cultivated and improved to the utmost, they might have enabled him to have cut a figure in the senate or as a scholar. He read with unusual rapidity, and evidently retained what he did read; for his literary acquisitions were surprising, considering the life of tumult he had led. He had always a quotation at hand from a Greek or Latin author, and there was a conscious feeling of ability about him, which he was somewhat wont to display. But, what says the poet?

"Without a genius learning soars in vain,
And without learning, genius sinks again;
Their force united crowns the sprightly reign;"

and here was this union wanting. He also wrote his

letters — to use a sporting figure — at the rate of twenty miles in the hour—generally at his dinner table, sending them out by his butler to be sealed, and very often to be directed, for he never had a secret in his life; and the letters he received remained for general inspection. I regret not having one of them to transcribe, but his off-hand addresses to his constituents, during his first contest for Shrewsbury in 1819, were particularly neat and appropriate, and were sent to the press before the ink with which they were written was dry. How much then is it to be lamented, that a man who had such resources for spending his life in the pleasantest, as well as the most honourable occupations, should have thus abused his mental powers, and subjected himself to misery of any kind beyond that which is common to all; and that repose and retirement, the secret wish of mankind, should by him have been considered valueless, if not irksome.

By the way, it is in my power to produce some specimens of Mr. Mytton's off-hand style of writing, in two of his addresses to the Freeholders of Salop, on his last unsuccessful attempt to become one of their representatives, in 1831; but they fall far short of the others both in matter and style. In fact they bear evidence of a mind in decay, and sinking with the general wreck.

ADDRESS (No. 1).

Mr. Mytton's first address to the Freeholders of Shropshire.—1831.

"To the Freeholders of the County of Salop.

"Gentlemen,—Domestic affliction of no slight or common nature has latterly limited my intercourse with you. My wishes for the prosperity of my native county have ever in absence held their usual sway.—Having once had the honour of representing your County Town in Parliament; feeling that various avocations precluded the conscientious performance of my duty to my Constituents, I declined the Representation at the dissolution of that Parliament. I have now no wife—no family—no hounds—no horses—(some will say, no steadiness of purpose)—but feeling that I can devote myself to your service, should you honour me with your support and confidence, I venture to offer myself to your notice as a Candidate for the County, totally unshackled by prejudice or otherwise, and a strenuous advocate for Reform.

"Relying upon the strength of the cause I shall advocate, I throw myself upon your favour, and shall assuredly take the sense of the county. I shall look to the vote of every Independent Freeholder, without making further professions.

"Your faithful friend and servant,

"JOHN MYTTON.

"*⁎* Peculiar private business may prevent my personal attendance, but I look upon it as a favourable omen—knowing that when absent you are best remembered.

"May 4th, 1831."

ADDRESS (No. 2).

"Friends! Men of Salop,

"In declining longer to continue the unequal contest in which I am embarked, I trust you will not consider my word forfeited. I have (and I trust with your approbation), come forward to assert the rights of freemen, and to break the bonds of tyranny asunder!

"Show yourselves the Proud Salopians!

"Gentlemen,—I pledge myself to come forward at the next Election for this great County, which I have already shaken to its foundation by my attempt to assert its independence, which shall be maintained with the vigour of a tiger, and the courage of the lion! Let your voice, as the Falls of Niagara, rush in force, and with the greatest velocity bear the fragile barks of corruption (which of necessity must be destroyed) to some land, perhaps at present unknown, but let them not be borne to the shores of Britain.

"I have asked no advice, — much has been offered, and maturely weighed, during this contest; but, Gentlemen, did I not feel myself capable upon reflection, of duly considering any subject which may fall under my notice, I should feel myself unworthy of looking for your approval. I came forth uncalled for, unprotected by any great interest; I retire from this contest in confidence of victory in future; I adopt one line of conduct, and from that I will not swerve.

"My thanks for the Unbought Votes of nearly Four Hundred Honest Men, are gratefully tendered to them;—the cause of Freedom in our devoted County will assume a brighter complexion.

"Gentlemen,-You will find me at my Post, the first

moment that a Reformed Parliament will allow it. My reception among you has, indeed, been proud; I beg to thank you for that exhibition of sincerely popular feeling in my favour, so strongly and so universally evinced.

"I tender my best thanks to the Ladies, for the smiles I have witnessed. Let me now intreat of you to allow the proceedings of Monday, to pass without riot or disturbance, as it would only entail disgrace upon the cause I advocate.

"I am, Gentlemen,

"Your Servant,

"JOHN MYTTON.

"Shrewsbury, May 14th, 1831."

Nor are the two following squibs by any means amiss. But Mr. Mytton's chance to represent his native county was slight indeed, having only polled 311 votes, the "proud Salopians," much to their credit, not by any means approving of the degrading association with which they perceived him to be leagued. There was a time, as I have before expressed myself, when he would have cut a very different figure at the poll.

Squib (No. 1).

"MYTTON AND BEARDSWORTH.

"An Electioneering Squib.

"Arrived last week in this Town, an old broken-down Racer, from the 'Union Repository,' Birmingham, with two BLACK LEGS, fresh fired and blistered. He is attended by an old Groom, grown grey in the Service, who has jockied him, UNBRIDLED, through many unlucky courses, and who, having lately considerably LIGHTENED his WEIGHT, flatters himself he will REFORM his style of running. The old Horse starts for the COUNTY STAKES this week; to be run for on the Quarry Course. The odds are 500 to 1 against him; nevertheless the Brums. (i.e., Brummagems) are in high spirits, he being backed by a few respectable branches of the MOB-ility here. Gentlemen are recommended not to go too near the Horse, he being vicious and apt to kick. It is understood, that should he not WIN, the Proprietor will take the Horse back with him to Birmingham, thinking to work him in a SLOW COACH and 'black jobs,' until he is fit for the nacker.

"Shrewsbury, May 9th, 1831."

Squib (No. 2).

"A Reform Candidate's Speech."

"Yes! gentlemen, upon my soul,
  I thank you much for what you've done;
Though at the bottom of the Poll,
  I've too much 'BOTTOM' yet to run.

"I told you all, when first I came,
  You'd not find ME the man to shirk;—
To play ON—now I've lost the game,
  Does seem like devilish up-HILL work.[1]

"'Reform's' my vessel, mann'd by Brums,
  Who hoist ME for their 'Union Jack';
She'll fight till Captain Beardsworth comes
  To steer her on some other tack.

"Yes! he has nail'd ME to the mast,
  Without a rag of CANVASS going;
And though we ARE capsiz'd at last,
  The Captain 'rais'd the wind' that's blowing."[2]

[1] Sir Rowland Hill, Bart., was the successful candidate.
[2] It is said that Beardsworth appeared on the hustings with a bank note, of large amount, pinned on his breast.

It is a great accomplishment to be able to tell a story well, but here Mr. Mytton did not succeed. In the first place, his sense of hearing was deficient, a great disadvantage in society. In the next, it was often difficult to determine whether he were in earnest or in jest, so fond was he of acting a part in the comedy of life. Again—he was very epigrammatic in his discourse, his sentences containing few words, and often leaving his hearers to guess what he really meant. All, however, was in the essence of good humour; and a more inoffensive companion, in the strict acceptation of that term, no man with his flow of spirits could possibly be. If in the moment of convivial mirth he let slip a word which he feared might wound the feelings of any person, he instantly made reparation, nor would he rest satisfied until it was fully acknowledged and atoned for. It is warmth of heart like this that distinguishes the friend from the companion and assimilates friendship to love. As to his politics, although he once was in Parliament, it would be absurd in me to attempt to decide what they were, for, during all the years I was acquainted with him, I never once heard him give an opinion upon the subject. It always struck me as not one of the maddest of his own acts, but certainly of his friends who encouraged him, to spend ten thousand pounds to obtain a seat in Parliament, in which he is said to have only sat half an hour, and to the duties of which he was by nature and habits utterly unfitted. I have reason, however, to believe—for I never interrogated him —he was what is termed a church and king man— in other words, at that period, a tory. But on this subject he was also full of his jokes. For example:—He had a famous race horse called Anti-radical; "but," said he when speaking of him, "I always call him *Radical* when he runs at Manchester."

Without appearing to care about it, or ever boasting of his success, Mr. Mytton was the best farmer in his part of the county, occupying between three and four hundred acres of land. Strange to say, at one of the Shropshire Agricultural meetings, he gained every prize for clean crops of grain, save one, a field of barley, his claim for which was rejected from a cause highly typical of the man. *It was found to contain "wild oats!"* As may be supposed, the report of the judge was the subject of much merriment to the company. His planting, as I before observed, was on a still larger scale, his object having been two-fold:—First, to replace the fine old timber, which he must have been aware would one day or other, fall under the axe; and, secondly, to form cover for the game, which, of course, he was resolved should exceed that of any other man in the country, and no doubt it did.

As a general sportsman few made themselves more conspicuous than Mr. Mytton did. He was many years a master of fox-hounds, (having kept a pack of harriers from his boyhood,) but his fox-hounds were not of a very high character. In fact to produce perfection in a kennel requires qualities the very reverse of his—namely, circumspection, perseverance, and patience. The establishment, as might be expected with himself at the head of it, was on a fully competent scale ; consisting of two distinct packs of hounds, and from twenty-five to twenty-eight horses. On Mr. Cresset Pelham relinquishing them, in 1817, he commenced hunting the Shropshire and Shiffnal (now called Albrighton) countries, five days a week; and continued to do so, with a fare share of sport, until the close of the season 1821 inclusive—making five seasons in all. His huntsman was John Crags (killed by a fall from his horse), and assisted by Edward Bates, son of Sir Richard Puleston's huntsman of that name, and Richard Jones, both very excellent horsemen and good men in their places. Mr. Mytton subsequently purchased another pack of fox-hounds, from Mr. Newman, of Hornchurch, Essex, which he hunted himself, about Halston, for several successive years, making up, by foxes purchased in London, for the confined country to which he was restricted.

As a horseman I need say little of Mr. Mytton, his merits having been proclaimed in every country in which he had hunted. In fact, taking him at every thing, he had not many equals and very few superiors in the saddle, for he could ride over a course as well as over a country. His prodigious strength was of great service to his horses, in proof of which they very seldom tired with him; and, making allowance for the seemingly impracticable fences he would ride at, he got but few falls. Considering his hard usage of them also, he was fortunate in his stud, several of his horses lasting many seasons; and his famous little one-eyed horse, Baronet, carried him nine seasons with hounds, after he had used him as a charger in the Hussars! Having, however, mentioned this gallant animal in connection with his hard riding master in my "Crack Riders of England," I will here quote what I there said of both. In speaking of the master, I say, "There[1] is no man better entitled to a place amongst hard, *aye, desperate* riders to hounds than Mr. Mytton is, and a welter weight too. But how is it that he can come under

[1] Vol. VII. page 89, New Sporting Magazine.

the latter denomination, who, ten or twelve years back, was riding amongst the gentleman jockies *under twelve stone ?* The question is best answered by the fact of his having been, by the aid of excess in good living, upwards of fifteen, with his saddle, for some years past; and I think Sir Bellingham Graham will confirm the truth of my assertion, that he was nothing short of that weight, on his capital Hit-or-Miss mare, when he so distinguished himself in that famous run with his, Sir B.'s hounds, of an hour and forty minutes, from Babinswood, in Shropshire. But it has not been in this run, nor in that run, in one country or in another country, that Mytton has made himself signal; and yet I might hazard an imputation on my veracity were I to recount *all* the extraordinary deeds of this most extraordinary man, in various situations with hounds. Indeed, adding the hazards for his neck that he has encountered in the field to those to which he has subjected himself elsewhere, the most extraordinary thing after all is, that he is at this moment in existence. However, confining my remarks to his riding, I am bound to pronounce him one of the most *daring* horsemen that ever came under my eye; and I must likewise add, that, all things considered, he has had fewer falls, and tired fewer horses in chase, than his larking and desperate system of crossing countries would warrant the expectation of. But this has been attributable to the immense muscular powers of the man; to a sort of iron grasp by which he holds his horses in his hand at all times, and upon all occasions, which, let your slack-rein gentlemen say what they may, is no small support to a horse going *his* (Mytton's) pace over a country, and particularly over the uneven surface, the deep ditches, and blind grips of his own county, Shropshire. Indeed, when I last met him, I asked him whether it had ever been his fate so to tire a hunter as not to be able to ride him home, when he declared he never recollected having done so. As to the height and width of fences which have been ridden over by him, I repeat I am afraid to recapitulate them; but I have very respectable attestation to my having once measured a brook[1] that he rode his famous one-eyed horse, *Baronet*, over, in cold blood, in my presence, and found it to exceed, by some inches, nine yards from hind-foot to hind-foot! But far from pleasing reflections are the result of looking back upon these brilliant feats of horsemanship, rarely excelled by any one. On the contrary, we cannot help lamenting that a person so gifted to shine in the field, as Mr. Mytton proved himself to be, should not have taken more care to preserve, unimpaired, the

[1] The Perry, which runs through the Halston estate.

Drawn and Etched by H. Aiken

Mytton on Baronet clears nine yards of water.

LIFE OF MYTTON

almost unequalled natural powers which he possessed,—so essential to the figure he made."

Nothing need be better than the shooting at Halston was—every species of game having abounded, as the following facts will prove. The average *annual* slaughter was—twelve hundred brace of pheasants; from fifteen hundred to two thousand hares; partridges out of number! There was also a good deal of wild fowl, and very excellent fishing. Mr. Mytton always made a point of killing fifty brace of partridges the first day of the season *with his own gun*; and I was once at Halston when he killed that number further on in the year. A neighbouring gentleman had betted him fifty guineas against the performance; but paid forfeit over night. This, however, did not satisfy the Squire. His fame as a shot was called in question, so he went forth with his keepers and performed the task in about six hours!

Barring Scotland, few gentlemen had better moors than Mr. Mytton had; and when I say that the annual income of his Merionethshire estate, on which they were, was £800, and that it consisted of little less than sheep walk, its great extent may be imagined, and consequently the extent of the moors. Thirty brace of grouse, was the average daily amount bagged during his annual visit to Mowddy,—or *Mouthy*, as it is pronounced,—where he had comfortable accommodations for himself and three or four friends. The right of Free Warren likewise gave him liberty over his neighbours' property, to a certain extent, and Mowddy itself is one of the few manors to be found in North Wales. The fishing here is likewise of the first description, and the mountain scenery not to be surpassed in the Principality. But, alas! although the mountains will stand fast till time shall be no more, this ancient patrimony has passed into other hands. It is to be hoped, however, that one day or another it may be redeemed.

But to return for a moment to Halston, and the feats of the trigger of the late owner of it and his friends. Amongst them, the two following may not very easily be exceeded. His brother-in-law, Mr. Walter Giffard, of Chillington, Staffordshire, now master of the Albrighton fox-hounds, and himself, took the field at eleven o'clock in the forenoon of a short and dirty winter's day, and between that hour and the dinner hour they bagged six hundred head of game from their own guns! On another occasion, an intimate friend of his and mine, together with himself, killed *a head of game every three minutes* for five successive hours! I state this "in verbo *sacerdotis*," so that the fact may be relied upon, but I withhold the reverend slaughterer's name.

It always appeared to me, however, that racing was more Mr. Mytton's passion than either shooting or hunting—and could he have been divested of that destroying spirit which accompanied him, he might have cut a very conspicuous figure on what may be called the country turf. He had the courage to purchase good horses,—for example, he gave three thousand guineas for Longwaist,—and his never failing memory enabled him to measure their ability by that of others in a manner that turned to his account. Previously, indeed, to the loss of his trainer and rider, William Dunn, who was killed by a fall in riding one of his horses at Chester, he had his full share of success; but it appeared to forsake him gradually after that period. The fact was, Dunn was not only an excellent trainer and rider, but he had some power over his master to restrain his running his horses to a stand-still, which he would do if left to his own discretion, and more for the sake of showing sport than from desire to win money. The sideboard at Halston exhibited thirteen gold cups, besides two silver ones, several of which were the trophies of one horse—the celebrated Euphrates, who, like one of the old sort, now become very scarce, continued running and winning to his thirteenth year! The expenses of his stud, however, must have been enormous, not only by consequence of its number, but his subscriptions to stakes amounted to an immense annual sum. He seldom refused to subscribe to any that were put before him, and the name of "John Mytton" often appeared as many as six times to the same. Of the science of breeding race horses he knew little or nothing; and the richness of the land at Halston proved a fatal obstacle to success.

His good nature and kind heartedness accompanied him everywhere, and particularly to the race-courses. He often started his horses without a prospect of their winning, for the purpose of affording sport—overruling the objections of his trainer, by saying—"'Tis a pity the country people should come so far from home and not have some fun."[1] In fact, that class of persons always built on diversion when "Squire Mytton's" horses were on the turf, and consequently, with them, the popularity of their owner had no bounds.

[1] Some years since, at Chester, he actually went to his stable and fetched a horse down to the course himself, which his trainer had not prepared to run, and, mounting his jockey at the post, won the prize contended for

"Which is *he*?" they would cry out to one of their friends that knew him. "That's *he*—that's *Mytton*," the friend would reply. "Dang it "— you would hear a Staffordshire potter or a Walsall nailer exclaim—"*ha looks loike a good 'un ; they tells me he can foight nation well.*"

Before he became too heavy, my friend occasionally rode among the gentlemen jockies [1] of the day; and here "John Mytton" appeared again, for strange to say, he did not like to see an intimate friend win, although he himself could not win. I had a rare specimen of this unaccountable frolic in my own person once, when riding in the same race with him at Lichfield. He knew he himself had no chance to win, but was determined I should not; and, by making several runs at my horse, caused him to break away with me in the race, and the little chance I had was lost by it. I say "the little chance," because, although I defeated seven of eight horses that started against me, by at least twenty lengths, the ninth came up and won cleverly at the last. This proved to be the famous Habberley, who was instantly purchased by Mr. Mytton, for two hundred guineas, but who had never started or been heard of before that day. He was

[1] Mr. Mytton's colours were green and white with a black cap.

called and entered as a cocktail, but, as his subsequent running proved, Eclipse was not more thorough-bred than he was; and no doubt the original owners of him knew it.

Let us here take a cursory review of his start and progress on the turf. It appears that he entered upon its fascinations at the earliest possible opportunity—viz., on attaining his majority, in 1817. In the book calendar of that year there are three horses attached to the name of "John Mytton, Esq.," the names of two of which, "Hazard" and "Neck or Nothing," are highly characteristic of the man, and especially so, at the commencement of his perilous career on this slippery ground.

He made his début at Oswestry on the 23rd of September, of the said year, on which day both the above named horses ran (Neck or Nothing breaking down); also a third, called Langolee, an Irish horse, purchased by him when in France, and which lasted him many years as a whipper-in's horse, and also was used in the stud, to get hunters.

In the following year, 1818, his name appears in the Calendar as owner of the following horses, Langolee, Leopold, Pranks, and Jupiter.

Langolee walked over for a hunter stakes and beat Mr. Jones's Kill Devil in a match at Shrewsbury, in September, which was his *blooding* of success on the turf. This year his horses ran at Oswestry (where "Captain Mytton" gave £50 to be run for by members of the Oswestry Yeomanry Cavalry), at Wrexham, Holywell Hunt, and Tarporley Hunt, over the new course on Delamere Forest.

In 1819 he had Jupiter, Sybil, Tamborine by Cervantes, Dot-and-go-one, Tattoo, Anti-Radical, Fox-Huntress by Sultan, and Single-peeper, in his racing stable; during which year, however, he experienced the want of success peculiar to most young turfites.

In 1820 his string of horses was considerably lengthened. In addition to Anti-Radical and Leopold, he had gr. f. by Fitzjames, Mandeville, Theodore Majocchi (late Handel), Halston by Langton, Claudius, Chance, The Polacca, George the Third, Brunette, Paul Potter, and Victorine.

Anti-Radical won him some good stakes at Chester, Warwick, Lichfield, Oswestry, Tarporley, and the gold cup at Manchester.

Mandeville won the gold cup at Nantwich and Nottingham, also 100 gs. at Manchester.

Halston won four stakes, value £200.

1821. Victorine, b. c. by Aladdin, Paul Potter, The Chancellor, Halston, Doctor, Anti-Radical, The Ruler, Vade-mecum, George the Third, Shrewsbury, Hudibras, Queen Caroline, Habberley, Single-peeper, Mandeville, Claudius, Theodore Majocchi were in his racing stable.

Halston won the gold cup at Nottingham, also stakes at Worcester and Chester, value 135 gs

Anti-Radical again carried off the gold cup at Manchester, also the Palatine stakes and the gold cup at Burton, and Habberley, then called Acastus, said to be by Shuttlecock dam by Gayman, gleaned some good things at the Anson Hunt, Manchester, Hereford, and Shrewsbury.

Mandeville also won four times, the stakes amounting to about 200 gs.

Claudius won the gold cup at Cheltenham.

LIFE OF MYTTON

1822. He had Claudius, Mallet, Habberley, Nettle, The Ruler, Enterprise, Queen Caroline Halston, Mandeville, Theodore Majocchi, Anti-Radical, Circe, Vade-mecum, Banker, two br. c.'s by Filho da Puta, Jovial, ch. m. by Milo, ch. g. by Young Alexander, Paradigm.

Habberley won the Billesden Coplow stakes at Croxton-park, the Half-bred stakes at Chester and Manchester, 40 gs. at Shrewsbury, and 80 gs. at Oswestry.

The Ruler, by Rubens, won the Sherwood stakes at Nottingham and £60 at Manchester. He was induced, by a flattering account given him by the owner, of a trial, to give five hundred guineas for this colt at two years old, worth about as many shillings.

Halston started ten times and only won £50 at Oswestry. Mandeville won 65 gs. at Nantwich. Anti-Radical 60 gs. at Cheltenham. Banker, by Smolensko, after he became Mr. Mytton's property (having been purchased this year of Mr. Charlton, with whom he had won the cup at Winchester), won the cup at Abingdon and 70 gs. at Shrewsbury. One of the Filho colts won 75 gs. at Lichfield. Jovial, by Go-

lumpus, won the Cocked Hat stakes at Shrewsbury
The ch. mare, by Milo, the silver cup at Oswestry.
The gelding, by Young Alexander, the Cocked
Hat stakes at Oswestry. And Paradigm, by
Partisan, the Wellington stakes at Basingstoke.

1823. We find Habberley, Banker, Enterprise,
Whittington, Euphrates (purchased of Mr. J.
Dilly), Libertine, Ostrich, Clansman, Paradigm,
Anti-Radical, br. c. by Bustard, Sir William
(purchased of Mr. Beardsworth), Cae Avon, The
Devil, placed after his name.

Habberley won the Bosworth stakes at
the Anson Hunt at Lichfield. Banker won
£60 at Buxton. Whittington, by Filho,
won £235 at Chester, Shrewsbury, Walsall,
and Stafford. Euphrates, then seven years
old, by Quiz, won the King's plate at Chester
and the gold cup at Worcester. Ostrich, by
Bustard (son of Castrel), won 183 gs. in two
sums at Knutsford and Warwick; and the colt
by Bustard won £90 in two sums at Oswestry and
Holywell.

1824. He had Habberley, Euphrates, Ostrich,
Oswestry, Berghill, Comte d'Artois, Whittington,
and Ludford.

LIFE OF MYTTON

Euphrates won the gold cups at Cheltenham and Lichfield, and the Oxfordshire stakes at Oxford.

Oswestry, by Filho, **won** £100 at the Pottery, £75 at Buxton, and the Mostyn and the Halkin stakes at Holywell. Berghill, by Bustard, won the Ludford stakes and £150 in three sums at Ludlow, Shrewsbury, and Wrexham. Comte d'Artois, by Bourbon, won £70 and the gold cup at Worcester, the gold cup at Hereford, and the Hawarden-castle stakes at Holywell. Whittington won the gold cup at Oswestry, the gold cup at Wrexham, another at Stafford, and £345 in different sums; while Ludford, by Manfred, won £50 at Holywell.

1825. Elizabeth, Cara Sposa (late Miss Fyldener), Ludford, Oswestry, Comte d'Artois, Louisa, b. c. by Amadis, Euphrates, Comrade, b. f. by Blucher, b. f. by Cannon Ball, b. f. by Ambo, Flexible.

Ludford won 100 gs. at Oswestry and Holywell. Oswestry won the gold cup at Shrewsbury and £55 at Burton. Comte d'Artois £60 at Shrewsbury. Louisa, by Orville, £225 at Chester, 70 gs. at Nottingham, and 100 gs. at Derby. Euphrates won the gold cups at Newton, Worcester, Lichfield, Wolverhampton,

and Oswestry, also £50 at the latter place.
Comrade, by Partisan, won 60 gs. at the Pottery.
The Blucher filly £225 at Holywell and £50 at
Wenlock. The Cannon Ball filly £50 at
Oswestry. Flexible, by Whalebone, £120 at
Shrewsbury, £50 at Oswestry, £210 at Holywell;
a pretty good year's work.

1826. Flexible, Whittington, Fisherman, Eu-
phrates, Balloon, Longwaist, Bowsprit, Louisa,
Ashbourn, ch. c. by Sam, b. c. by Amadis,
Harriette Wilson, Lark, and Comrade.

Flexible won the Darlington cup at Wolverhampton and £70 at Cheltenham. Whittington
£60 at Chester. Euphrates carried off the gold
cup at Lichfield, the gold cup and £50 at Oswestry,
the King's plate and £70 at Chester. Longwaist,
by Whalebone, won the gold cups at Newton,
Buxton, Worcester, and Warwick, also £40 at
Chester. Bowsprit, by Rainbow, won £50 at
Ludlow. Ashbourn, by Cheshire Cheese, £60
at Oswestry. Colt by Amadis, £230 at Nottingham; and Harriette Wilson, by Manfred, £40 at
Shrewsbury.

1827. Fisherman, Flexible, Lechmere, Ellesmere, Halston, Euphrates, Mexican, Lark.

Ellesmere, by Filho, is the first winner of the above lot, viz. of £125 at Nottingham. Halston won £275 at Chester, £175 at Ludlow, and the Chillington stakes at Wolverhampton. Euphrates won the gold cup and £50 at Oswestry, and the King's plate at Lichfield. Lark, by Rubens, £55 at Nottingham.

1828. Spruce, Hedgford, Euphrates, Halston, b. c. by Master Henry, The Crofts, br. f. by Filho.

Spruce, by Skim, won £100 at the Anson Hunt. Hedgford, by Filho or Magistrate, the cup and £50 at Chester and £50 at Nottingham. Euphrates won the cups at Ludlow, Worcester, Oswestry, and Wrexham, also the King's plate at Chester. Halston, the Palatine stakes at Chester, 100 gs. at Newton, 75 gs. at Worcester, 200 gs. at Burton, the Avon stakes at Warwick, 155 gs. at Oswestry, the Taffy and Pengwern stakes at Holywell.

1829. The numbers were considerably reduced. Brown filly by Filho, The Crofts, Halston, Hedgford and Euphrates, being the whole of the horses he had in training.

The Crofts, by Whalebone, won £125 at Oswestry

and £50 at Wrexham. Halston, the Tradesmen's cup at Chester, the cup at Knutsford, £350, the Pengwern stakes, and £115 at Holywell. Hedgford, £63 at Chester. Euphrates, the gold cups at Ludlow and Wolverhampton and the King's plate at Lichfield.

1830. This year brings us to a close, Halston and Hedgford being the only race horses he had left. The former winning £50 at Holywell, and the latter the Cheshire stakes at Chester, £110 at Newcastle, and £50 at Wrexham.

I find I must here retrace my steps a little— and this for two reasons. First, I shall follow the good example set by himself in bearing testimony to the worth of a good servant; and secondly, shall transcribe a letter of his own, which sets forth the writer of it in his true character. It will be recollected I asserted that Mr. Mytton's success on the turf somewhat declined after the death of his trainer and rider, William Dunn. Let it not be supposed, however, that I intend in the least degree to disparage the good conduct or abilities of his subsequent trainers or riders, but to impute it to that "tide," as Shakespeare calls it, in every man's affairs, wherein fortune has a share, which, despite of every thing and every body, will now and then set against him. I have good reason to believe that Mr. William Dilly and my old servant, Thomas Horsley, did all that could be done for Mr. Mytton as trainers of his horses; and the fair ability of his jockey, Whitehouse, is very generally acknowledged. His master's opinion of him, however, is here unhesitatedly given in one of the *prettiest* letters—if I may use such an epithet—that I ever perused.

"*To the Editor of the Salopian Journal.*
"Sir,
"Having lately heard it asserted, as the general opinion, that the defeat of my celebrated horse, Longwaist, may be attributed to the dishonesty of his rider, I feel called upon, as his owner, to express my most firm and unshaken confidence in his integrity, till now unimpeached, and in truth unimpeachable.

"Nothing but anxiety to rescue the fame and character of a highly valued servant, and deservedly admired rider, would induce me to trespass on your valuable columns; but feeling that the character of Whitehouse is as unspotted, and as valuable to himself as that of the highest of our nobles is to him, I cannot resist making my confidence in his worth and integrity thus public:—

'Who steals my purse steals trash; 'tis something, nothing;
'Twas mine, 'tis his, and has been slave to thousands:
But he that filches from me my good name,
Robs me of that which not enriches him,
But makes me poor indeed.'

"I am, Sir,
"Your obedient servant,
"JOHN MYTTON.[1]
"Halston."

As a pendant to the above I may here introduce the following tickler that he wrote to the Editor of the Old Sporting Magazine in the spring of 1831, in answer to some observations that had been made about Mr. Beardsworth and the horse Birmingham.

"GUY STAKES AT WARWICK.

"SIR,

"IF there is one thing more absolutely requisite than another in a letter which is intended for the public

[1] The following is a copy of his Autograph—strongly indicative of the rapidity with which he used his pen on all common occasions.

eye, it is accuracy; or, to speak more plainly, Truth—a qualification that your Correspondent, THE YOUNG FORESTER, has in your Magazine of this month (February) unhappily overlooked.

"In page 247, he says, 'The Stake at Warwick has been awarded to the owner of Cetus, who was second, in consequence of the present owner of Birmingham having refused to pay some paltry £25 forfeit for a stake at Winchester, where the horse was engaged in the name of the person whom Mr. Beardsworth bought him of.'—This is notoriously untrue; and, by the manner in which the writer speaks of the transaction altogether, it is to be feared it is wilfully so.

"The next paragraph I apprehend too is incorrect; but which I will not speak so positively about, because I know but little of racing, and therefore am unwilling to compete with so precocious a youth as this appears to be.

"He says, 'It has long been one of the best acknowledged rules of racing, that no horse is entitled *to be a winner* until all the arrears due for such animal

have been paid up.'—Is he sure of that?—
Where is the rule to be found? Has he not
made a mistake? and instead of the words
'to be a winner,' should he not have said
'to start'?—This talented gentleman may not
see the difference. — Great wits, they say,
have short memories — perhaps they are short-
sighted too!—In my humble judgment, there is
a great deal of difference. By making use of the
word 'start,' you afford the owner an opportunity
of paying the stake in arrears *if applied for*, instead
of letting the *onus* hang over his head till he has
defeated his antagonists.

"And now I would ask, did Sir Mark Wood
'most honourably' make any application to the
Stewards or Clerk of the Course before Birmingham started at Warwick for the paltry £25
forfeit at Winchester? THE YOUNG FORESTER
answers this question partly, asserting, 'he
apprized both trainer and master, previously to
the race, of the objection he had to make.' Now
if he had done so, I should say they (that is, the
trainer and master) were not the proper persons to
apprise. The Stewards (or at all events the Clerk
of the Course) were the proper persons; but, unfortunately for THE YOUNG FORESTER'S veracity, here
is another untruth: Sir Mark Wood did *not* 'most

honourably' apprize Mr. Beardsworth (the owner), previously to the race, of the objection he had to make.

"'Save me from my friends,' he says, 'has been the cry through many ages:' but, instead of Mr. Beardsworth echoing it, I guess the Jockey Club and Sir Mark Wood are more likely to apply it to this doughty genius, and conjure him, if he is determined to attempt to take their part, that he will assert only that which is true.

"I am, Sir, your humble servant,

"JOHN MYTTON.

"Halston, Feb. 19, 1831."

A summary of Mr. Mytton's actual racing career may be comprised in a few words. He had too many horses in the first place, and too many of them not good enough to pay their way. It is evident he was anxious to have good ones in his stables by the prices he gave; but he bought several, of that sort, *after their day was gone by* — for example Count d'Artois, Banker, Longwaist, &c. &c. He had however several good winners — old Euphrates at their head; and Whittington, Oswestry, and Halston were esteemed very "smart" horses in the racing world. Indeed it is believed, that, in some hands, they would have been trump cards. As for himself, as a racing man, he was too severe upon his horses; they rarely came out fresh, after Chester and one or two other places; and therefore, this fact admitted, he had, I think as much success as he could have expected. He seldom backed his horses to any serious amount; *generally* not at all.

His stables were, as has been before stated, upon Delamere Forest, in Cheshire, and he had at different times for training grooms — William Dunn (also his rider who was killed); Maurice Jones, one of the old sort; William Dilly, and Thomas Horsley. Jones had always one answer to his master's question—" Shall we win this race, Maurice?" "Well I can't say, indeed, sir; but *I think we shall be nigh handy, please God.*" His home stud-groom, Tinkler, was also one of the old sort—a careful nurser of young racing stock, but too fond of green meat to contend with young horses of the present day. Mr. Mytton never bred a good race-horse.

This anecdote of Maurice Jones reminds me of another. I was once on a visit to the late Mr. Bayzand of sporting notoriety, when he received a letter, en-

LIFE OF MYTTON

closing a bill of expenses for training, from "old Sadler" as he was called, father to the present Isaac. It contained the following postscript.—" I have had a terrible summer of it; won nothing; but *by the blessing of God,* hope to do better next year."

When speaking of Mr. Mytton's conduct towards his two wives, a delicate hand is required; for the mind naturally revolts from retracing, circumstantially, any thing intimately connected with the sacred compact between man and wife; but—as the reader will perceive—I should fail in my object, in writing this memoir of my departed friend, if I shrank from the arduous and painful task. I need no justification for the performance of it; I find it, first, in the fact of the notoriety given through the public journals, to the proceedings in Chancery, on the final separation of the late Mr. Mytton from that amiable lady who is now his widow; and, secondly, in numerous misrepresentations that have gone forth to the world, which, to the utmost of my ability, I shall endeavour to clear up. I wish, however, for one sip of Lethe now, and that my readers could partake with me of the same cup; for, as in criminal law, good character bears no weight against positive evidence—at least, as regards the verdict returned—so I much fear the numerous virtues of my old friend will not here more than balance the account, unless large credit be given him on one score. The follies of mankind are familiar to our view, and we can always find an excuse for *them*; but it is difficult to account for that evil principle which prompts a man to give pain to a woman whom in his heart he loves, and whom he has every earthly reason to love. "*Sic visum est diis,*" 'tis the will of the gods, said the ancients—a poor excuse, if not a little blasphemous; and I should rather lay it to poor human nature, who sometimes exhibits herself in most mysterious guises, as was the case here, accompanied by errors and failings over which — as we are not permitted to command oblivion — delicacy and humanity would fain draw the veil.

But this painful part of my subject—if my end is to be attained — will not admit of concealment, and the evil must at once be laid bare to our view. I reluctantly admit, that Mr. Mytton's conduct in the marriage state is in great part indefensible, and can only be *palliated* by a due allowance, which must not be denied him, for that sort of insane delirium under which he so frequently laboured—no matter from what cause—and to which so many of his otherwise unaccountable acts —not the acts of John Mytton, *per se*—can alone be placed. Delusion is the true character of insanity; and when I say that great part of his unjustifiable, and, by the world, I fear, hitherto unpardoned, treatment of two of the most exemplary and virtuous women in existence, was jealousy, nothing more need be said to establish this point. What says the poet? and beautifully has he said it,

> "It is jealousy's peculiar nature
> To swell small things to great; nay out of nought
> To conjure much; and then *to lose it's reason
> Amid the hideous phantoms it has formed.*"

In the case before us, not only the groundlessness, but the unreasonableness of his suspicions were such as could have emanated from no sound mind, which never dreams of effects unconnected with a cause; and this is nearly the sole mitigation I have to offer for one of the greatest blemishes human nature can sustain. On this point he was mad; on others, only eccentric; but — as has been falsely said of wit — "thin partitions do *their* bounds divide." The fate of each of these ladies, however, has been a hard one. The one dropped into an early grave; the other would have been torn from him by her friends, had she not made up her mind to abandon him, lest, like

Semele in Jupiter's, she might have found her death in his embraces.[1]

But, setting aside this monomaniasm, what further extenuation have I to offer? I answer—as regards his second lady—none, save madness. His first and himself were not well assorted. She had been nursed on the lap of refinement and fashion, to which her betrothed was a stranger, and was by consequence ill calculated to be the wife of a rough country squire, who had never been at Almack's in his life, and who had something like a sovereign contempt for all such exclusive association. Nor was this all—and should any young female's eye rest for a moment on this page, let it well observe, that it may well mark, one

[1] So tender is woman's fame, that the very *breath* of calumny will taint it. It behoves me then to say, that, in their situation as wives, two more correct in their conduct might have been searched for in vain, than the ladies I am now alluding to. Any man but Mr. Mytton would have been proud of exhibiting them in public, but had they lived in the days of Pericles, or even been the wives of the Great Mogul, they could scarcely have been more secluded than they were at Halston. Not even a race ball would he let them be present at, for some years of his life! To what motive but jealousy, or, what is worse, *suspicion*, could such conduct be attributed. In justice to the deceased husband, however, I must state, that the health of the first Mrs. Mytton was very delicate when she was married, which may account for her premature death.

rock on which thousands of her sex have split, and which she to whom I am alluding did not steer clear of. *The first Mrs. Mytton conducted herself with coldness to her husband's old friends and companions, the sons of the native gentry of his neighbourhood, in every respect her equal.* To a man of Mytton's temperament, to whom an old friend was "as the core of the heart, or the apple of his eye," this could not have been without its effect, and on one occasion is said to have drawn tears from him, during a dinner party at his own house; and from my knowledge of the man, I doubt not the fact.

There is a readiness to believe ill reports without examination into their truth, and we are often found guilty by those who will not trouble themselves to look into the accusation. Is all true, then, that has been reported, and credited by too many, of Mr. Mytton's conduct to his first wife? Certainly not. Fame loves to double, and the world is not only credulous, but loud, and too often scurrilous, in its censure. Not content with the various embellishments of vulgar rumour, absolute falsehoods were in general circulation; and amongst them the following: — He was accused of having thrown her lapdog—curse those lapdogs, married woman have no business with such pests — upon the fire; but fortunately for the memory of my departed friend, the act that gave rise to the vile report I myself was a witness to. He merely took it up in his arms, threw it half way up to the drawing-room ceiling, and caught it, without injury, on its descent. The butler (who happened to be in the room at the time) called out, "Oh, Mr. Mytton, you'll kill the dog," and the lady screamed and cried; and on this was the dreadful charge founded. In the hilarity of high animal spirits, Mytton was much given to practical jokes, as all his friends know. Thus, on the same lady once accompanying him to the kennel, he shut the door upon her for an instant, after he himself had got outside of it, and this was magnified into his wishing, or, I believe, *intending*, that she might be devoured by his fox-hounds. Again — he threw her into deep water! Nonsense; he was never mad enough to do that. He merely, one very hot day, pushed her into the shallow of his lake at Halston, a little over her shoes. All this was, no doubt, wrong by a young lady who had been brought up so tenderly as Miss Jones had been reared, but with a hundred young ladies I could name, who had been differently treated in their childhood, nothing would have been thought of it, beyond a joke. And then we should look at the man. If, independently of his own immediate connexions, he had a greater regard for one person than for any other, I have reason to believe it was for his Halston chaplain, and he was two or three times nearly being the death of him—once absolutely confining him to his bed for several weeks, from the consequences of his having, by way of a "lark," knocked him over some iron railing at his hall door at Halston. Cruelty was not the property—no, not even the excrescence, of his nature; although, in his practical jokes, I admit he was rough, judging perhaps of other people's corporeal feelings by his own.[1]

I have said he was without excuse for ill conduct to his second wife, and I must again say, *why*. Not merely is her beauty the weakest of her charms, and her disposition and temper most amiable, but all who knew her will join with me in saying, that if a wife had been selected for Mr. Mytton with a view of reclaiming him, and making him a domestic character and a kind husband, she might have been the woman fixed upon for the experiment. Like Terence's lover,

[1] How many times have I overheard such remarks as the following, made on Mr. Mytton, by ladies, in my hearing, in distant parts of England—and indeed now and then nearer home. "Oh! *he is a brute!* He threw his wife's dog on the fire and burnt it alive! He tried to drown her, and wanted his hounds to eat her alive." Pshaw.

then, he should not only have sworn never to have forsaken, or unkindly treated her, forasmuch as she was the object of his choice, and *had been with difficulty obtained*; but there was that suitableness of temper (the "*conveniunt mores*" of the poet), which the one valued so highly, and the other had not, perhaps, met with before. In short, there was every prospect of happiness from this union, and for some years indeed it appeared to be realized; but whether it was that he once again nursed a vulture to feed on his own heart, or whether it was not in his nature to live comfortably for any length of time with a woman, however suited to his taste, and however dear to his heart, is a question not to be resolved by man. He has, certainly, been exhibited as a pattern of ruffianism in his conduct towards this amiable lady, and as some detail of it has already been before the public, a repetition would be useless, as well as painful to the humanity of my readers. But here comes the paradox. He loved this woman to distraction; he would have given the apple of his eye for her at any time; he would have risked twenty lives to have gotten her back again, and obtained her forgiveness; he raved about her in his madness; and sent her his dying benediction! Were those brutal deeds, then, the deeds of the kind-hearted John Mytton— kind to every living soul but the woman whom he loved to distraction! Oh, no; they were the deeds of a man visited by the hand of the Almighty, afflicted with a distempered brain, *a monomaniac beyond all doubt.* Could he, then, like Scylla, have got an Act of Oblivion passed in his favour for this sad stain on his, otherwise, good name, he would perhaps have passed even an earthly tribunal. But how fortunate is it, O man!—and especially for you who may be the loudest to condemn him —that we have reason to hope there is more mercy in heaven than in this, often too reproachful world.

But is it possible, it will still be asked, that Mr. Mytton could have really loved either, or both of his amiable wives? Indeed, reader, he did, and, woman-like, despite of his conduct they both loved him. Neither did they reproach him. He could not complain with the noble bard—

"Though my many faults defac'd me,
 Could no other arm be found,
Than the one which once embrac'd me,
 To inflict a cureless wound?"

But he might have joined his brother exile in his plaintive song—

LIFE OF MYTTON

> "All my faults—perhaps thou knowest,
> *All my madness*—none can know;
> All my hopes, wheree'er thou goest,
> Wither—yet with thee they go."

And I speak from experience on these points. In the fatal illness of his first wife, I obeyed the call of friendship, and went to him at Clifton Hot Wells, where she died, and I can vouch for his sufferings on that occasion. Who that has ever seen him look upon her portrait at Halston, and speak of her afterwards, could doubt the truth of what I have asserted? And yet, could they both rise from their graves, and were he to meet her again in all her beauty, and with all her charms, as he had met her before on their bridal day, I would not answer for many years of domestic happiness—even with the experience of the past to boot. "What is passion," says my Uncle Toby, "but a wild beast?" and unless restrained by reason, or subdued by temperance, it is as furious and violent as the brute beast himself. We may throw a gem to a cock or a pearl to a swine, but each would be better pleased with much humbler fare sought for and selected to their wild taste and pleasure; and I need not apply the moral here. It has been shown beyond a doubt, that it was not in the power of woman—no, nor in the power of himself—to have made John Mytton a good husband; indeed he ought not to have entered into the marriage state at all.

We must then still proceed in the catechetical mood. How could any woman venture on Mr. Mytton, as a husband, after the publicity given to the history of his proceedings towards his first wife? I answer—In the first place, many of the evil reports in circulation were found to be untrue. Secondly, there was a great intimacy, as well as congeniality—if I may apply the word here— between the brothers of his second lady and himself, who could see nothing but what was congenial in their brother sportsman and friend. Again— Why was Venus (the Egyptian one) represented standing naked, on a lion, but to indicate that love conquers even the fiercest beast? Here then was the lion in toils. The suing lover was on his very best behaviour during the days of probation, to which I was myself a witness, for he often made my house his home, as it was within two miles of that of the object of his choice. Again, "*Credula res amor est.*" Love believes every thing; and not only the young lady—and young she was, for, if my memory serves me, she was only in her seventeenth year—but we all believed there was a fair prospect of happiness in the anticipated union. Neither was it suffered to take place without due consideration. The *pros* and the *cons* were nicely weighed and weighed again by the anxious mother, and they appeared nearly to balance the scales. Still it was long before her mind was made up, and in the intimacy of our friendship she put the following home question to me :—" Had you a daughter marriageable," said this amiable lady, and exemplary pattern of a wife and mother,[1] "would you like to see her married to Mr. Mytton?" I very well remember my answer, which was this:— "In my opinion, Lady Charlotte, Mr. Mytton has no business with a wife at all; but should he marry your daughter, Caroline, there is a greater prospect of his making a good husband to her, than to any other woman in the whole world." Now not only did my words prove true, but for several years he *was* a good husband, and had it not been for "the grave of reason" which excess in wine became to him, as indeed it does to most other men, I doubt not he would have continued in the same course. But what an exemplary wife was Miss Caroline Giffard to him! How well did she bear her seclusion from society; what allowance did she make for his libertine life; how much did it cost her to estrange her heart from him who had stamped it with its first impression! " I cannot help loving him with

---

[1] Lady Charlotte Giffard, sister to the late Earl Courtney, of Powderham Castle, Devon.

all his faults," said she, to me one evening at Halston, after recounting some of his acts which only a madman would have committed ; and were my life to endure a thousand years, I could never lose my recollection — unless I lost my reason —of that distressing scene. But it is true, thought I, as I listened to the sad tale, what is said of woman—that Heaven is pleased to make distress become her, and dresses her most amiably in tears.

But independently of conduct towards herself, there were other circumstances which must have been the source of much pain to this amiable lady. Nothing is more precious to a woman's heart than the good name and credit of him she loves. The unfortunate connexion then between Mr. Mytton and the person I have before alluded to, sank deep in that of the lady in question, and well might it have stung her honest pride to the quick. The best of men is not free from human infirmity ; but of all the vices short of what is termed "the great offence," to which *a gentleman* can be addicted, nothing so far debases and lowers him in the eyes of all who have an interest in his welfare, as his quitting the rank to which he by birth belongs. 'Tis the last step to a general dereliction of all gentleman-like feelings and a sorry compliment to his former friends. "Tell me with whom you associate," said the sage, "and I'll tell you what you are," was one of the noblest lessons, if not the severest rebuke, ever given to mankind. It is the voice of custom, echoed by the voice of reason.

I have but little to say of Mr. Mytton as a father, but that little is in his favour. He was very fond of his children, although, as may be expected, he had a peculiar way of showing his affection for them — such as tossing them in the air as he did the lap-dog; giving view-holloas in their ears at a very tender age, throwing oranges at their heads, and all such practical jokes; but as the brute said of the eels he was skinning, it was "nothing when they were used to it," and I think his conduct towards them was nearly *sans reproche*. He often spoke of them in his exile; and when he came in contact with other persons' children, about the age of his own, a close observer would detect the workings of a strong inward feeling which it was not in his power to conceal. But why should he wish to conceal it? there is a chord in the breast of a savage that responds to the voice of nature! John Mytton himself could alone answer this question; but as a celebrated character in antiquity wished for a window in his breast that every one might see into it, a peep into that of this extraordinary man would have exhibited qualities and virtues which not only the world refused to give him credit for, but which he himself seemed resolved it should not believe he possessed. Strange and unfathomable man! Hypocrisy is the homage which vice pays to virtue; God knows you paid her nothing in *that coin*; you seemed determined to make us think you kept no account with her at all!

PART III

I HAD not seen Mr. Mytton for at least two years previously to my quitting England, but I had heard some unpleasant reports touching his pecuniary affairs; yet it was not until I read the advertisement in The Times of the sale of *all* his effects at Halston, that I found his race was run. As the greatness of every man's fall is measured by the height from which he fell, my heart bled as I waded through the melancholy detail of objects so familiar to my mind, so dear to himself, and also associated with brighter days of my own. "Poor fellow," said I, to a mutual friend who was at my side; "better he had never lived, than to have to taste those bitter moments which in future must be his portion. He who towered like the cedar will now be trampled upon like the bramble, and perhaps neglected by those whom his bounty once fed." What became of him, however, after the sale of his effects at Halston — for every thing was sold except Euphrates, the race-horse — it is not material to inquire; and I only know that, being in fear of arrest by creditors, he sojourned for some time at a small hotel in Richmond,[1] from which place are to be dated circumstances and events deeply affecting his future, short, but melancholy term of life.

On the 5th of November, 1831, during my residence in the town of Calais, I was surprised by a violent knocking at my door, and so unlike what I had ever heard before in that quiet town, that, being at hand, I was induced to open the door myself; when, to my no little astonishment, there stood John Mytton! "In God's name," said I, "what has brought you to France?" "Why," he replied, "*just what brought yourself to France*; (parodying the old song) three couple of *bailiffs* were hard at my brush." But what did I see before me? The active, vigorous, well-shapen John Mytton, whom I had left some years back in Shropshire? Oh, no! compared with him, 'twas the "reed shaken by the wind"; there stood before me, a round-shouldered, decrepid, tottering *old-young* man, if I may be allowed such a term, and so bloated by drink that I might have exclaimed, with Ovid,

---

[1] Before going there, I believe he was a good deal at one of the fashionable bachelor hotels in Bond-street, where he might be seen sitting down to dinner, with bailiffs, money-lenders, and ragamuffins of all descriptions, who haunted and followed him wherever he went.

"Accedant capiti cornua, *Bacchus eris*."[1]

But there was a worse sight than this. There was a mind, as well as a body in ruins; the one had partaken of the injury done to the other, and it was at once apparent that all was a wreck. In fact, he was a melancholy spectacle of fallen man — of one, over whom all the storms of life seemed to be engendered in one dark cloud.

After drinking some wine, he took his leave of me, abruptly, saying he was going in a carriage to Guines, a small town eight miles from Calais, where he had been quartered, when in the Hussars, with the army of occupation; but, taking me affectionately by the hand, said, "I shall come to you to-morrow, for I have a great deal to say to you." The morrow came and he himself came, accompanied by Mr. Vaughton,[2] and I hope neither of us may have occasion to witness such another scene. His pecuniary affairs appeared not to give him a moment's uneasiness. As regarded them, fancy, or something worse, had dressed the future prospect with the gayest colours; he had seventy

---

[1] If you had but horns on your head, you would be Bacchus.

[2] A brother sportsman from Warwickshire, at this time residing in France.

thousand pounds to receive, he said, after all his debts should be paid; had engaged McDonald, the jockey, to be his trainer and rider of his new stud of race-horses; and had purchased a capital house in Curzon-street, May-fair, where of course there were a knife and fork for me, and bail for ten thousand pounds! Neither did he appear to care two pence for what had occurred at Halston. It was to be reinstated in its former splendour, and once more was I to be his guest. It would have been cruel to have undeceived him here. Like the good citizen of Argos, he might have upbraided us for so doing, and exactly in his words:—

"Pol me occidistis, amici,
Non servâstis," ait, "cui sic extorta voluptas,
Et demptus per vim mentis gratissimus error."[1]

But the sore was not yet laid bare. A very elegant writer has observed, "there are some strokes of calamity that scathe and scorch the soul, that penetrate the vital seat of happiness— and blast it, never again to put forth bud or blossom;" and this we could perceive was his case. He was writhing under one of them— *the madness of wounded affection,* and though

[1] It would have been better, my friends, that you should have destroyed me, than to have deprived me of the most agreeable delusion of the human mind.

vanquished, he would not yield. "I'll have my wife back again, by G—d," said he; "*look at these marks*," pointing to a wound on each wrist, which it appeared he had purposely kept from healing; "*they handcuffed me*;[1] but, so help me G—d, I'll have her yet." Here a violent hysterick affection put an end to the scene; but it was evident that not only had the "iron entered into his soul," but that the foundation of his happiness was sapped, and that, in his then course of life, either his reason or his health must give way.

One week's experience of his proceedings—for he was never sober throughout the day—confirmed me in the above view of his case, and I thought it my duty to take some precautions. The first step was to interrogate his valet, as to what instrument he had in his possession by which he could put an end to what—if he ever suffered himself to take a clear and sober view of it—must have been a barren and cheerless existence; and the next, to inform his friends of my fears.

[1] He alluded to a desperate attempt he had made to regain possession of his wife, after she had returned to her family at Chillington Hall; when it was found absolutely necessary for the constables to handcuff him, before they could make themselves secure of his person. It has been stated that he knocked down eight persons in the rencontre. No doubt he went "big with daring determinations," but he was foiled by a good look-out.

LIFE OF MYTTON

Barring his mother, his uncle, Mr. Owen, of Woodhouse, near Shrewsbury (one of his guardians), was his nearest relation; to whom I stated my apprehensions that his nephew would either go mad, or die, and very shortly too, and wished for his advice as to how I should act in case my suspicions should prove well grounded. His answer as regarded myself was kind, and that of a gentleman; but as concerned his nephew it was conclusive. He had never, he said, taken his advice in any one instance, therefore he declined offering it on the occasion on which I sought it, and muchsoever as he lamented the ruin that had befallen him, it was a consolation to him to reflect that he had not in the smallest degree contributed to it. (This letter is dated November 25, 1831, just twenty days after his nephew's arrival at Calais.)

It may be easily imagined that the arrival of my old friend at Calais, in the state in which he then appeared, was any thing but what I could have desired. My pen was at that time employed on a very interesting subject, and I knew, from past experience, how many times in the day I should be interrupted by him. But I had shared his prosperity, and I was not going to desert him in his adversity. He did not, however, want for society at Calais. He gave dinners at his hotel; and as Epicurus's wise man would cultivate friendship, as he would the earth, *for what it produces,* there were plenty such wise men to be found in Calais.[1] This, however, was not the worst of it. Still wiser men followed him from London, as I shall straightways take occasion to show, as also how fortunately their designs were frustrated.

Although my house, with its humble fare, was always open to Mr. Mytton, I never made one of his dinner parties; but one evening, about nine o'clock, he came into my dining room, accompanied by a man, in a rough great coat, whom he introduced as a livery-stable keeper in Edgeware-road, but who, in my eye, had every appearance of a London thief. On hearing Mr. Mytton say something of a draft or bill, I asked this person what was the amount of his demand on Mr. Mytton, when he replied, "under £100." To cut this story short then, I shall only state, that I cautioned my friend against giving bills in a foreign country, and also requested his old acquaintance, Mr. Longden, then residing at Calais, also to caution him

[1] Here the character of the man appears in its true colour. One gentleman, previously unknown to him, borrowed his coat, with the Anson hunt button on it,— rather unceremoniously, as he said,—to go to a ball. He ordered his valet to line the gentleman's own coat sleeves with fish hooks against he called for it, the next day.

—for our suspicions were equally aroused—but we were both equally repulsed with "mind your own business," or words to that effect; and the rascal succeeded, that evening, after he left my house, in getting his signature to a bill for £200!! And even this was nearly being not the worst of it. A gang of swindlers, of which this fellow was one, were in the town with stamps suitable to £5,000, for which amount they *intended* to get him to sign bills, with the promise of remitting him the money for them.[1]

But this was only the commencement of that memorable evening's work. After repairing to the hotel, where the bill was signed, Mr. Mytton and his *friend* sallied forth to a " finish," and somewhere about midnight, returned to the hotel, and now comes the climax.

But, reader, one word with you first. You have heard, no doubt, of many memorable deeds performed by fire. You have read that somebody set fire to Troy, Alexander to Persepolis, Nero to Rome, a baker to London, a rascally Caliph to the treasures of

---

[1] The payment of this bill was stopped by placards in the streets of London, in which the names of other gentlemen who had been swindled by the same party appeared.

Drawn and Etched by H. Alken

"D—n this Hiccup!"

Persepolis, and the brave Mucius Scævola to his own hand and arm to frighten the proud Porsenna into a peace; but did you ever hear of a man setting fire to his own shirt, to frighten away the hiccup? Such, however, is the climax I have alluded to; and this was the manner in which it was performed: "D—n this hiccup," said Mytton, as he stood undressed on the floor, apparently in the act of getting into his bed; "but I'll *frighten* it away;" so seizing a lighted candle, applied it to the tail of his shirt, and—it being a cotton one—he was instantly enveloped in flames.

Now, how was his life saved? is the next question that might be asked. Why, by the active exertions of his London customer, and of another stout and intrepid young man that happened to be in the room, who jointly threw him down on the ground and tore his shirt from his body, piecemeal. Then, here again comes John Mytton! "The hiccup is gone, by ——," said he, and reeled, naked, into his bed.

It is easily to be supposed that the irregular life Mr. Mytton was at this time leading had its due weight with his valet, and, although he had been some four or five years in his service, he had left him that night to his fate, and was pursuing his own pleasures in Calais. The following morning however, between the hours of seven and eight, he came to inform me of what his master had done, and wished me to come instantly to see him. " What doctor have you got ? " said I. " *None*," replied the man. " Send for Dr. Souville immediately," added I, " and I will come to your master as soon as I am dressed." [1]

Shall I ever forget the scene this morning presented ? There lay Mr. Mytton, not only shirtless, but sheetless, with the skin of his breast, shoulders, and knees of the same colour with a newly-singed bacon hog. He saluted me, as usual, with a view holloa, but I told him that was no time for joking, and asked him *why* he committed so silly an act, and one that might very probably be the cause of his death ?—in fact, had the flames caught his body one inch lower down, his intestines would have been burnt and he must have perished ! His answer was — the answer of a madman—that *he wished to show me how he could bear pain.* The scene closed with the arrival of the doctor, who applied the usual palliatives, but whose

---

[1] Our eminent English physician, Dr. Bradley, was at this time absent from Calais. Dr. Souville, however, is the principal French physician, and of acknowledged **practical ability.**

opinion as to the result, it was then almost useless to ask for.

Any man but John Mytton, would have tried to have aided the exertions of his doctor, to alleviate sufferings which very shortly became severe, but he absolutely added fuel to the fire. The more he smarted the more he drank, but, like the Spartan boy, he never squeaked. "Can't I bear pain well?" he would say to me six times in the day, and in truth he did bear it well. But although it sometimes happens that the spirit is willing, whilst the flesh is weak, here the flesh was the stronger of the two, for the mind of the sufferer very soon became affected. I have, however, omitted to mention one act he committed the day after his accident, which, if committed by any other man but himself, would have been evidence to have shown that he was already mad. "Is not —— going to dine with you to-day?" said he to me. On my answering in the affirmative, he observed, that I might have asked himself to have met him. "It would cost you your life," resumed I; "you must be stark mad to think of going out in the state you are at present." He gave me one of those looks which generally implied mischief, and which were well understood by his friends; but said nothing more at the moment. Just after we were seated at our dinner, however, in walked John Mytton; but although he sat out the meal and half an hour besides, he fainted twice, and was glad to return to his bed. But even this is a trifle to what he afterwards did. He had been five weeks in his bed, when he declared he would dine with me on New Year's day. Nothing but the straitwaistcoat would have restrained him, and he came; and moreover, because there were not four horses to the carriage, to take him back to his hotel—not three hundred yards—he would walk, without even a great coat, but supported by two persons, and although the air was cold and damp he was not a whit the worse for it. What would some people give for such a constitution as his, and how difficult was it even for him to destroy it!

Of all the uncertainties of our present state, said Dr. Johnson, the most dreadful and alarming is the uncertain continuance of reason; and although there may be "a pleasure in madness madmen only know," it is harrowing to the feelings of others to behold it. My prediction respecting Mr. Mytton was fulfilled; he became to a certain extent deranged in about a fortnight after the burning, and it was quite evident he would very shortly become a maniac. Symptoms at length gave apprehension of his becoming at times dangerous; the straitwaistcoat was ordered, and the men were in readiness in the house to apply it. "Wait," said I, "and let me try, once more, if I can arouse him to a sense of his situation"; and entering his chamber alone, the following conversation passed :—

"Mytton," said I, "I come to tell you that your doctors assure me you will be a corpse in three days, unless you give up drinking brandy." "So much the better," he replied, "I wish to die." "That is not the speech of a man of your good understanding," I observed; "you may yet see happy days if you will give up drinking brandy. Will you promise me you will give it up?" He said he would not; but on my telling him there were men in the house ready to put his person under restraint, he said he would promise to drink only what his doctors might allow him; and this was all I wanted. The keepers and the waistcoat were dismissed.

His mind soon experienced the benefit of this wholesome change, but the irritation from the burning brought his life into peril. In fact, Dr. Souville told me he did not expect him to live, apprehending typhus would ensue; and, as an old Warwickshire brother sportsman[1] who saw him said of him, "no other man but Mytton would have survived." He would faint on being moved from his bed to his chair, and he had every symptom of sinking nature. Under these circumstances, I had a duty to perform which I did not shrink from, but never should I have dreamt of making public the result, were it not that I consider it honourable to the man, and it cannot fail of being satisfactory to his friends. Sitting opposite to him, then, by the fire-side, I thus, in pain, addressed him. "I think it right to tell you, your life is in danger; I know you too well not to be convinced that you will not scoff at what I am going to suggest. Would you like to see our clergyman, Mr. Liptrot? He is a liberal-minded, worthy man, without an atom of humbug about him." "Draw your chair by the side of me," said Mytton. On my placing it on his right, he requested me to place it on his left, and to sit myself down upon it; when putting his left hand into mine, he struck his breast violently with his right, and with as much vehemence as in his then weak state he could command, exclaimed—"I never intentionally injured any person in my life, and I hope God will forgive me." These words were followed by a flood of tears; yet how exactly do

[1] Mr. Henry Wyatt.

they resemble those of Manfred to the Abbot of
St. Maurice :—

> "I hear thee. This is my reply; whate'er
> I may have been, or am, doth rest between
> Heaven and myself—I shall not choose a mortal
> To be my mediator."

The offer of sending for the clergyman was declined, but without further remark.

Cicero says, no man in his sound mind is quite destitute of religion; and even unsound as poor Mytton's—to a certain extent—always was, I am quite sure he was not destitute of it, although his proud spirit was loth to own a dread of any thing, either human or divine. But supposing he had never owned it to man, we are not to imply that he did not own it to his God; for although the fall of Solomon is told, we know nothing of his repentance. I shall have occasion, however, to show that the subject of this memoir was a sincere, though perhaps a late penitent, and I rejoice at having it in my power to do so, as I should have been sorry to hear that he "died and made no sign."

There is a scrap of Latin which has often met my eye, and is as often applied to nations as to individuals, but I cannot say I know the author of it. "*Quos Deus* (or *quem Jupiter*) *vult perdere, prius dementat ;*" which is as much as to say, that those persons whom the Almighty wishes to destroy, he previously causes to grow mad (which is, I believe, the literal and only meaning of *demento*, a word not in use in elegant Latin). I know not on whose authority the conduct of man's Maker is thus, I think, impiously speculated upon; but should a fiat so dreadful have been really pronounced, let us hope it will plead in favour of some of the acts of poor John Mytton, for which, with a heart like his, nothing short of madness could possibly account or justify.[1]

[1] It never before fell to my lot to watch the motions and actions of persons labouring under a temporary aberration of the mind, much more to receive letters from them. Amongst the numerous ones which my poor friend wrote me in that melancholy situation, the following convince me that, however discordant may be the instrument of thought (the brain) at the time—though some keys may jar, there are others which yield the usual tones to the same touch:—

"Dear Ramrod (for Nimrod),

"You shall not stay longer with old Jack Longden in my sitting room, but come up stairs to see a Hero, late Chillington, die the death of a saint." Here was the ruling passion, strong even in madness and in death, for he was very ill at the time. Hero was the name of a famous hunter he bought of me, which he afterwards called Chillington; and he married a daughter of the ancient house of Chillington. There were as many as half a dozen dashes under some of these words.

LIFE OF MYTTON

On the morrow of the day on which I had the conversation with Mr. Mytton on the serious condition in which he then appeared placed, he asked me, as he lay in his bed to get a sheet of paper and write what

Again, there was the following; in which the fatal passion for the Circean cup—that cup which, like Nabal's, turned a heart of flesh to a heart of stone—too plainly appears.

"Dear Ram.,

"Jam satis terris nivis atque diræ grandinis misit Pater, et, rubente" porto. Here goes a bumper to old Ram."
Signed "John Mytton."

This extraordinary production is dated "the Gallies," and directed thus :—"Fall at a rasper! To Mytton's best friend." The quotation from Horace is worth notice, inasmuch as every word is rightly spelled, the punctuation correct, and the capital "P" in Pater, as in the original. There were six dashes under the word "rubente" and four under "porto," but the inverted commas ceased at "rubente!" The following postscript was added to it.

"Nummi si nolo custodi rendere vinctus
Præmii num mi (eheus miseri!) restat ahenea turris?"

"Prison or not to prison—can it be a debt, as it's not self-contracted, non sponte suâ, nec voluntate meorum filiorum." Here it appears his Latin is not quite so correct, but he alludes to the impression, that he was not aware on what account his liberty was denied him. This last epistle was succeeded by another the same day, which shows that the brain became more disturbed. "Dear Ram. H—l to pay—come here instantly, they are all found out—*poison*. Ever J. M." I have a hundred such notes, the dates of all which I marked, and I suppose Mr. Roberts, the proprietor of his hotel, had as many. On perusing several of them, I could have exclaimed, with Shakespeare,

"Oh, what a noble mind is here o'erthrown!"

he dictated. I did so, and it consisted of the following lines:—

> "Condemn'd in youth to meet the grave,
> I hope to be received above;
> Render my soul to Him who gave,
> My latest breath to you, my love."

He then requested they might be placed in his view on the door of his chamber (where they remained for a considerable time); "and," said he, "when I die, I trust to your sending them to my wife." I told him I would do so; and had he died at that time, I should certainly have complied with the request.

It would be both useless and tedious to describe the various scenes that passed in the chamber of my poor friend, who was guarded day and night by three persons at a time, after he recovered his strength; but some of these scenes would put the powers of description at defiance. His conversation, for example, with these persons, who were English smugglers, was at times ludicrous in the extreme, and highly characteristic of the man.[1] Previously to this precaution,

[1] There was nothing that medical skill or humanity could suggest left untried to relieve the sufferings of Mr Mytton. Several of his friends sat up, or lay on a spare bed the whole night in his room, and of course I took my turn. It happened one night, that I was accom-

however, rather an awful scene was witnessed by me. A servant from his hotel came to inform me that Mr. Mytton had got six carving knives in his possession, and was by himself in his room. Mr. Vaughton and myself entered it, and such we found to be the case, with the trifling difference that only two of the six were carving knives, the other four being dinner or case knives. He was lying on his bed with the six knives in his hands, when I placed myself at its side, and Mr. Vaughton—a very powerful man—stood at the foot. "Heyday, Squire," said I, "what are you going to do with all those knives." "Come and lay down by my side," said he, "and I'll show you (of

panied on my watch by a waiter from some hotel in London, who was sent over to Mr. Roberts's hotel for the purpose of learning the French language. "Nimrod!" exclaimed Mr. Mytton; but I feigned sleep. "Nimrod!" he repeated, "I want to *talk* to you;" but I was still asleep. "Come then," said he to the waiter, "sit by me, and talk to me. You have heard of my hounds?" "Your hounds, sir," said the man —a thorough-bred cockney; "I can't say as I ever did." "Why, you d—d fool, where have you lived all your life? Did you never hear of Euphrates?" "I can't say as I did, sir," replied the man. "What!" said Mytton, "*never heard of Euphrates the race-horse!* I'll have you smothered to-morrow, by G—d. Get back to your great chair, and go to sleep!" This reminds me of an anecdote, related by Boswell, in his most amusing Life of Dr. Johnson. The Doctor was asked how he liked his attendant (a stranger), who sat up one night with him, in his illness? "Not at all;" was his answer. "The fellow is an idiot; he is also as awkward as a turnspit when first put into the wheel, and as sleepy as a dormouse."

course I begged to be excused); I have made your fortune and old Vaughton's too—a hundred and fifty thousand pounds apiece for each of you—for I have found out that *these knives will extract fire from flesh.*" "Ah," said Mr. Vaughton, "but how much better would they do that if they were *warmed at the fire.*" "To be sure," replied our poor deluded friend; and giving them into his hands, they were soon put outside the door. Now it will no doubt appear a mystery in what way these knives could have been procured, and well it may. But will it be credited that they had been given to him by his own servant, of whom I had only a few weeks before required possession of every thing—even to his nail-knife—by which a wound to his person could be given. Such, however, was the case; and it is scarcely necessary to observe, that the man was from that hour forbidden to come near his person, and soon afterwards was discharged.

The effects of education on first-rate talent shine forth when little expected, as was the case with this extraordinary man, even when his mental aberrations were nearly at their height. In one of his paroxysms he talked eight and forty hours without ceasing, and, as it may be supposed under such violent excitement, a recollection of last year's clouds would not be more difficult than a record of the unconnected jargon which he at that time uttered. But in his calmer moments, when he saw me by his bed-side, he would quote Greek and Latin authors with surprising readiness, and when he found he was incorrect would pause until he recovered the text. In several of these quotations it was beyond doubt apparent, that the bereavement of his family and the desolation of Halston were present to his mind ; for in some particular instances I could not be mistaken. In giving that beautiful passage from Sophocles, wherein Œdipus recommends his children to the care of Creon, I am quite certain he was applying it in his mind to the first-named calamity ; and an epigram from the Greek Anthologia, on the fall of Troy and the death of Hector, which he would very often repeat, had a sympathetic allusion to the ruin at Halston and his own fall. But the following criticism could scarcely have been expected from a mind in ruins. In reply to the numerous messages he would send to the bar of his hotel, some answer was generally to be manufactured, and "master has not got such a thing in the house," was by no means an uncommon one. It happened one day, however, that the attendant in waiting brought him what he had sent him for, but delivered it into his hands with the usual announcement—"Mr. Roberts *hasn't* got *no*

such thing, sir,"—he having procured it elsewhere.
"Why," said Mytton, looking the man in the
face, in my presence, "you are a Greek." "No,
sir, I ar'n't," he replied. "But I'll be —— if
you are not," continued Mytton, "for in Greek
two negatives make the affirmative stronger;" and
roared into his ear "χωρὶς ἐμοῦ οὐ δύνασθε ποιεῖν
οὐδέν, says the Bible." The fellow stared, and well
he might; and well indeed might Mr. Mytton's
uncle say, as he did in his letter to me, when
lamenting his nephew's situation and contrasting it
with what it might have been—" Heu, ubi lapsus!"

But we will bring this scene to a close.
Having reason to believe that, either by his
powers of eloquence or by the force of that
sympathy in a British sailor for the absence of
grog, which is inseparable from his character,
and will be a formidable opponent to Temperance Societies on the coast, he had prevailed
upon one or two of these otherwise honest guardians
to procure him spirits by stealth,[1] it was determined
by Mrs. Mytton, his mother,—who had for some time
been in painful but unremitting attendance on her son
—that I should proceed to London and state his case

[1] He would at this time frequently send for eau de
Cologne, under the pretext of using it as perfume, or
otherwise externally, on his person. We soon, however,
by the quantity consumed, ascertained that he drank it!

to Dr. Sutherland, as, in fact, we were making no progress towards recovery. The result was two experienced attendants being sent to Calais, by whose skilful treatment an alteration for the better was soon apparent, and their patient able to take his airings in a carriage. It is, however, somewhat singular that the only time that it was found necessary to put my poor friend under absolute personal restraint, was during the time I was absent from him, in London, and on my return—John Mytton like—he spoke of it as a very good joke.

The scene now changes again, and somewhat of a brighter prospect appears. Although Mr. Mytton had every comfort, as well as every convenience at the Royal Hotel in Calais,—the landlord of which, Mr. Roberts, is a person of superior education and conduct, and was much esteemed by his unfortunate guest—yet when it was considered that he had been occupying the same apartments so long, in sickness and in sorrow, it was desirable, on the approach of spring, that he should breathe a purer air, and a chateau was looked for in the neighbouring country. But here arose a difficulty. The few persons who had such things to let were alarmed at the idea of *a gentleman and his keepers*, and fearing the occupation of them by such tenants might leave a stain on their premises, refused to let them on any terms. What then was to be done? His removal to England would have been his removal to a prison; so, at the request of Mrs. Mytton, I consented to hire a chateau and to receive him as an inmate until his recovery was completed. But I went beyond this: I undertook to make a trial of managing him myself, without the aid of his keepers, and the first ten days bade fair for success. He conformed to regular hours; enjoyed his meals; did not exceed his bottle of light wine; was, I thought, never happier in his life, and the recruitment of his health was beyond all expectation. But luckily for all parties, at the request of his mother, who was gone to England, his keepers still remained in Calais to await the issue of the experiment, for at the end of a fortnight he stole away to Calais unobserved; got at the brandy bottle, and then it was all over with my "brief authority." It was with great difficulty that I could prevail on him to return to dinner for three successive evenings, and on the fourth he was outrageous, threatening to murder a gentleman at table, who had been most kind to him in his illness. It then became necessary to send to Calais for his keepers, and by eight o'clock the next morning, with the advice of his doctors, he was under their care.

Provision was made for this somewhat anticipated change. The chateau afforded ample accommodation for the whole party; but as, in all such cases, it is necessary to separate the patient from persons and objects which are sources of mental excitement, Mr. Mytton and his attendants had apartments separate from mine, and which were arranged in the most convenient manner for all purposes of safety. The attendance of these young men acted like a charm upon their patient, who recovered his former serenity on being told that he was *again* placed under the surveillance of the police for striking a Frenchman in Calais. But let all those whose constitutions are the worse for wear by indulging in midnight revels, and strong drink, and who may take a glance at the Life of John Mytton, mark and digest what I am now about to state. When he left the town of Calais he was gradually recovering his strength of body and mind, but was very feeble on his legs, and could scarcely enter a carriage without assistance. He had not been at this chateau a month, before, by regular living and daily exercise in sea air, he was able to walk six or seven miles in the middle of the day without the slightest fatigue, and to take a walk in the evening besides. His meals were eaten with a relish, and without the aid of Cayenne pepper, to the use of which he before knew no bounds; and his sleep was tranquil and refreshing. Now methinks it will be asked—how did he employ his time? Why, painful but striking is the answer to this question. He to whom the whole world had appeared insufficient to afford pleasure, and who had spent hundreds of thousands of pounds in pursuit of it, was now completely happy in the occupation of picking up sea shells in the morning and washing them in vinegar in the evening!! So eager was he in this his favourite pursuit, that he would scarcely finish his dinner before he would enter upon the last-mentioned office, and would absolutely stand for two or three hours at a time brushing shells with a nail brush dipped in vinegar! They were then laid with great precision in drawers, which he would never suffer any one but himself to open. All this, with the perusal of the Morning Herald, the Age, and the Calais (French) Journals, formed the business of the day.

It is almost needless for me to state that, at this period, the intellect of my friend was in a state of great imbecility — the consequence of extreme exhaustion, produced by extreme excitement. Nevertheless it was the opinion of his attendants, as well as of Drs. Souville and Winder, who saw him two or three times a week, that, by pursuing the plan they were then acting upon, he would in time recover his strength of mind as well as that of his body; and there also was a chance—as his old friend and neighbour in his own county, Colonel Proctor, then at Boulogne, observed—of his altering his former course of life, from the experience he might have of the benefits arising from temperance and exercise. But alas, poor man, this chance was denied him. At the end of the second month he was, by false representations made to his mother, once more let loose, and from that hour to the last of his life his poor shattered bark was never out of a sea of troubles. He had nearly been suffocated with brandy on his voyage to London, by the steamer, the day after he left the chateau; and, as was evident to all parties, so soon as he was caught in England he would be in a jail! Why then was he taken to England? and why was his life thus suffered to be sacrificed? Why, merely to enable him to sign deeds conveying away the last remaining acre of his unentailed property, which he could not do when in the situation from which he was taken, and which, it appears, when done, did not secure his person from the griping fangs of the law. He did sign them, however, and his own death warrant by the same act and deed. There might be other reasons for getting him to England, which it may perhaps be unsafe for me to commit to paper; to my mind they were conclusive.

I shall take but a bird's eye view of his career in England, but, carrying on the allegory, we may compare his situation to that of small birds pursued by hawks. Every bailiff in London was on the look out for him; and, above all places in the world, he went to Halston to avoid them! Oh, what must have been his feelings on the first view of his deserted hall—the scene of all his former splendour! They must have somewhat resembled those of "The Last Man," when viewing the capitals of the world, and himself alone left to mourn over them; but as they are incommunicable by words, I leave them to the imagination and likewise to the sympathy of the reader.

>   ("Such a house broke!
> So noble a master fallen! All gone! and not
> One friend to take his fortune by the arm,
> And go along with him;")

Let us hope, however, that he was neither sober nor in his senses — at all events, that some respite was in mercy granted to his intellectual faculties, as a guard to his heart, from the assaults of sufferings that might otherwise have been beyond man's nature to endure!

But his stay here was short; he was hurried off to Shrewsbury jail, whence, in the course of time, he was removed to the King's Bench prison, in London.

Now here again comes "John Mytton"! During his sojourn in the first-named prison he was visited by several of his old friends,—influential gentlemen in the county—who offered their services in arranging his difficulties, provided he would put his affairs into their trust, but he rejected all their overtures. Either Cæsar or nobody he was resolved to be so long as he was above ground, and how exactly did he come under that denomination of persons of whom Horace speaks,

"Quem neque pauperies, neque mors, neque vincula terrent;"

and how plumply did he give the lie to the adage, that adversity is the school of reform. The toad was ugly and venomous; but *he* saw no "precious jewel in his head."

But there was something savouring of the serio-romantic in Mr. Mytton's being placed in durance, for debt, in the prison of a town with which the deeds of his ancestors were so deeply and brilliantly associated

—in a town in which his word would but a short time before have been good for ten thousand pounds, and in which he once sat high in the people's hearts; and also in relation to the altered situation in which he himself once stood towards the keeper of that prison. The governorship becoming vacant, the contest for it was a severe one, and it was solely by the influence and exertions of Mr. Mytton that the present person, Mr. Griffiths, fills it. He, however, not only has done credit but honour to his benefactor's choice,—as no man in Shrewsbury is, I believe, more respected than he is, neither can any man exceed him in the various and arduous duties he has to perform, tempering mercy with justice; and although Shakespeare says, "seldom when the steeled gaoler is the friend of man," Mr. Griffiths was unceasing in his kind attention to his patron, now become his prisoner. Indeed Mr. Mytton not only acknowledged this to me, but told me he was very comfortable in Shrewsbury gaol!

On a writ of certiorari being executed, my poor degraded friend was conveyed to London in the custody of Mr. Griffiths, and transferred to that of the Marshal of the King's Bench, where I saw him for the first time since he left the chateau in France.

But what a change for the worse was here! He was the same bloated, unhealthy-looking, son of Bacchus that he appeared on his arrival in Calais, and he had a leg in a state nearly approaching mortification. In fact, his surgeon told me he would owe his life—at all events the preservation of his leg—solely to the kindness of a fellow prisoner, who prevented his drinking spirits, and such no doubt was the case.

I am not able to say how long he remained in the Bench, but on his exit John Mytton— *unus ex omnibus*—appears again; but to what account shall we place the act I am about to mention, for it appears to me to want a name? It is not, however, without a plea. The heart of man has been elegantly compared to a creeping plant, which withers unless it have *something* around which it can entwine; but towards what a frail trellage did that of this extraordinary man yearn for its support! Walking one day over Westminster-bridge, the following dialogue occurred between himself and a female of a class which the reader will not be at a loss to name, but on whom he had never before set his eyes.

Mr. Mytton. "How do ye do?"

The Female. "Very well, I thank ye; how do you do?"

Mr. Mytton. "Where are you going?"

The Female. "I don't know."

Mr. Mytton. "Then come and live with me? I'll settle £500 a year upon you."

Here was no law's delay; no worm in the bud; no concealment feeding on the damask cheek, but love at first sight, if any love there was! The bargain being struck, the broomstick jumped over, the happy couple soon afterwards arrived at Calais, at the Crown Hotel; Mr. Roberts, under such circumstances, being compelled to decline the honour of their company. But the strangest part of the affair is to come. This young woman, then only in her twentieth year, whom no doubt some scoundrel had seduced and abandoned, was not only possessed of considerable personal charms, but proved to be very respectably connected,[1] and conducted herself towards her pro-

---

[1] The late Lord Arundel, who was at this time sojourning at the Royal Hotel, on his road to Italy, confirmed to me the respectability of her connexions on hearing their names mentioned.

tector so much better than could be expected, considering whence she was imported, and that his lusty love had gone "in quest of beauty" and not "in search of virtue," that I saw a letter to her from his mother acknowledging her kindness towards her son. But wife or mistress made no difference with Mytton. If he were not, generally speaking, a madman to a certain extent, on the subject of a woman—*and, above all, of a woman he loved*—he was a monomaniac, and some extraordinary scenes were the fruits of this extraordinary connexion. The green-eyed monster played his part as usual, and at times a nod or a look was suspicion strong as holy writ.

I must hark back here for a moment. On the morrow after Mr. Mytton arrived from London, he was arrested for £25 at the suit of the holder of one bill out of four for £25 each, which he had been most improperly induced to accept in favour of a person resident in Calais, who had not the slightest claim upon his liberality, and conveyed to the prison of the town. His solicitor being then with him, there was no difficulty in releasing him to the extent of that individual sum, but it was considered expedient to detain him in custody until it could be ascertained what was become of the three other bills; when it was at length agreed that two of them should be given up, and that his liability only extended to £50. Here then will appear the character of the kind-hearted John Mytton, in its true light. Almost any man but himself would have been outrageous at this breach of confidence and good feeling, but not so John Mytton. The first step he took after his release from the prison, was to call upon the person who had caused him to be thus disgraced, and to walk arm in arm with him on the market-place—lest, as he said, the affair might injure his character in the town, he being a professional man. Reader; I'll bar you from one book, and one book alone; you shall then search the pages of ancient and modern history, and I challenge you to produce me a nobler instance of a nobler heart than the one I have now given you. The power of bearing and forbearing, which constituted Epictetus's wise man, comes, perhaps, next to it in theory.

But the storm soon gathers again. After sojourning a certain time at the Crown Hotel, in Calais, with a score to his name of a thousand francs, he came to my house in the country to inform me he should go to England on the morrow. It was in vain that I told him he could not do so without first paying his bill, which I knew he had not, at that time, the means of doing. He, however, put himself into the Boulogne coach the next afternoon, meaning to embark from that town—having, perhaps fortunately, informed the barber who shaved him of his intentions, which intentions the barber of course conveyed instanter to the landlord — and the following day found him in Boulogne jail. Also luckily for him, his agent arrived the same day, but his creditor had previously agreed to release him, on an undertaking from Mr. Roberts, of the Royal Hotel, and myself to bring him back to Calais. The distraining landlord has since paid the debt of nature; but he was quite free from blame with regard to the steps he pursued; and Mr. Mytton was kind as usual to him on his return.

Shortly after this, Mr. Mytton and his chère amie took their departure for Lisle; but what they did at Lisle I did not trouble myself to inquire. Their return to Calais, however, forms another interesting scene in this — I know not what to call it, but perhaps the ancient Greeks would have called it—δρᾶμα τοῦ βίου, or *comedy of life.* Just as I was sitting down to dinner one evening of a very hot day in August, I espied a person at the bottom of my avenue, approaching my house on foot. "Is it possible," said I, "that person can be Mytton?" Mytton, however, it was; and shall I ever forget the state he was in—shirtless, waistcoatless, neckclothless, with his trousers and coat stained with blood, as well as in a state of very great exhaustion from fatigue? Now then for his account of himself. He had set forward, it appeared, in a diligence from Lisle to Calais, but had quarrelled with Susan (his chère amie's name) at St. Omer, and refused to proceed in her company any further. When she left him behind at St. Omer to proceed to Calais, he had nearly four napoleons in his pocket; but getting into a street-row in that town, he had been well licked and robbed [1] of all save three Belgic sous. With this small sum he started to walk to Calais, twenty-seven long miles, and under a burning sun; but becoming dead beat before the sun set, he put up at a small public-house, or cabaret, by the road side, and the account he gave of his proceedings in it, was a most ludicrous one. He wheedled the old woman, he said, out of some supper; but then what was to be done for something to drink? "Why," continued he, "I can leave part of my clothes in pawn in the morning, so got two glasses of gin and water, gin being cheaper than brandy." On refreshing himself at my house, and

[1] I should rather say he had lost this money out of his pocket.

putting his person into something like a decent condition, he walked into Calais, and made it up with Susan.

The comedy is now at end — at least for the present — and something very like a tragedy succeeds to it. Poor Mytton was, a few days after, again arrested for £200, being the amount of the score he had run up at a certain French hotel in London, where himself and his partner had been sojourning after the bargain had been struck on the bridge, and from whence he had been obliged to bolt in a hurry, as the bailiffs were in the house in pursuit of him. But the landlord, being a Frenchman, had recourse to the privileges of a Frenchman, and I once more was pained by seeing my friend looking through the bars of a French prison window. Here he was suffered to remain—the why and the wherefore can only be answered by his solicitors in London, as the sale of his estates had been completed—for *fourteen days*; on the thirteenth day, I thought it my duty to inform his mother of his situation; and in four days from the date of my letter she was in Calais. It would be painful to me to relate, as well as to my readers to be made acquainted with, a detail of the acts and deeds of this unhappy man during the rest of the time he spent in Calais, where his mother remained to protect him as far as it was in her power to do so. But it was brandy, brandy, brandy, morning, noon, and night, which of course drove him to madness; and a disposition to insult the French people, made it necessary to remove him. England was again determined upon, where not only a prison, but the grave, yawned to receive him, and in a prison he died. Thus fell John Mytton — by nature, what God must have intended every man should be; by education, or, rather, from the want of *proper* education, nearly at last what man should not be. The seed was good; but it fell among thorns and was choked.

So soon as I was informed that Mr. Mytton was once more within the walls of the King's Bench Prison, I felt assured he would never quit them but on his bier, neither did he. But as the poet says—

"Better to sink beneath the shock,
Than moulder piece-meal on the rock;"

and I was happy when I heard the fatal subpœna had arrived, for adversity had exhausted her phial, and it was evident that, with the exception of the unsubdued affection of his mother, there was, for him, no balm in Gilead. It appeared that in about three weeks after his incarceration, he was seized with paralysis of the extremities, which bade defiance to the treatment of Doctor Maton and Mr. Brodie, who indeed from the first considered it a case without hopes. It may be, however, a consolation to those who had a regard for him, to learn that his sufferings were not severe; that his mother was by his bedside at the last, and that as he had been conversing rationally with his medical attendants within half an hour of his decease, his life must have departed like the flickering flame of a lamp which goes out by the last crackle. But it is astounding to think, from the rapidity with which his lamp of life must have burned, that he lived to complete his thirty-eighth year. As I said of him before, *Nil violentum est perpetuum;* Phaeton's car went but a day!

A brother sportsman and a brother prisoner (well known at Melton Mowbray) who, as I have before mentioned, had been extremely kind to my poor friend during his first and second incarceration, and who was a constant attendant on his sick bed, wrote me — unsolicited — some interesting particulars relating to his illness and the last scenes of his eventful life, which it gives me pleasure to make known. The "virtue of suffering well," which Johnson allowed to Savage, could by no one be denied to Mytton, whose bearing and forbearing, as I have before shown, are perhaps not exceeded by any man's; but in the opinion of his friend he took much to heart this second confinement in the King's Bench, although his proud spirit would not suffer him to acknowledge it; and he thought it hastened his end. As to his dying in peace with all mankind, how could he die otherwise who never attempted to revenge himself on any human being, but who — though his communication was not "Yea, yea, or nay, nay" — so far from demanding the eye for the eye, and the tooth for the tooth, would have actually given his cloak to him who stole his coat—whose heart was as warm as those of half the world are cold; and whose warmth of heart had brought him into the prison in which he died! And how did he die?—As he *appeared* to live — in dread of nothing human or divine? Certainly not; although it may, tauntingly, be said, he trusted to the delusive support of a death-bed repentance. Let no man, however, venture to pronounce sentence here, but leave it to that bar at which justice will be tempered with mercy; where, unless I formed a very erroneous opinion of the late Mr. Mytton — and who had a much more intimate knowledge of him than myself?— and a still more mistaken one of the attributes of Him by whom he will be judged, he will find acceptance before many who have carried a much fairer face to the world. Few receive the white garment and carry it without a stain before the judgment-seat. John Mytton certainly did not: it was soiled and stained with the impurities of our nature — with even more than can be placed to that account—and the world has no proof that they were attempted to be washed out by his tears; but I appeal to my own experience of him—to that of his brother prisoner and friend who attended him in his last days—in the hour indeed when the heart knows no guile, and in which the tongue seldom hazards an untruth, whether he did not then own to man, what he had previously only owned to his God. Although it appears he did not consider his life in imminent danger, he had the church service read to him nearly every day, and more particularly on Good Friday, when he held a long conversation with his brother prisoner on the sacrament, but which, although he expressed himself very properly in his allusions to it, it does not appear he partook of. Of both his wives he spoke in the tenderest terms of affection, as also of his children by each, and expressed a strong desire to see his present wife and *all* his children together—but alas! that wish was a vain one. Immediately after his decease, a cast was taken of his features by the celebrated phrenologist, M. Deville, in the Strand, at the express request of his mother, in which *it is said* the character of the man is very clearly developed.

The first public notice of his decease that reached this country was contained in a very neatly written paragraph in the Globe, in which the following short, but just character was given him:—"His princely magnificence and eccentric gaieties obtained him great notoriety in the sporting and gay circles, both in England and on the Continent. His failings, which leaned to virtue's side, greatly reduced him, and he has left numerous friends to lament the melancholy fact of his dying in a prison, which, contrasted with his former splendour, furnishes a striking illustration of the mutability of mundane affairs." This account went the round of the papers, with the exception of Bell's Life in London, which inadvertently stated that he had spent the fortunes of two wives, but which the editor immediately contradicted on my authority. That of his first, which was ten thousand pounds, was settled on his only daughter by her; what his second wife's fortune was, I never heard, but whatever it might have been, I have reason to believe it remains for the benefit of his younger children.

It is too much the practice of the world—at least so

says the satire—to adore the rising sun, and to condemn him when going down; but neither errors nor *crimes* (if such, reader, you will have them) nor adversity, could chill the grateful recollection of the splendour that had once illumined Halston, and of the many, otherwise, perhaps, sad hearts which had been warmed by its genial rays. But even independent of this, there was a tenderness and compassion of nature in both the sayings and doings of poor John Mytton, which had fixed him firmly in the hearts and affections of the people within many miles of his house, and there he remained fixed to the last. In proof of this, his funeral excited very general, indeed, I might say, almost unequalled sympathy. The amazing number of three thousand persons were present at it—several appearing unable to stifle their feelings, and only obtaining relief by their tears. And what brought together this assemblage of persons of all conditions, even to the poorest? Not, as Shakespeare says, to

> "———————— tender down
> Their services to Lord Timon ; his large fortune,
> Upon his good and gracious nature hanging."

No—but to shed a tear on the bier of a man whose "large fortune" and whose "gracious nature" were no more; of a man who had died in a jail; of one who, with "all his imperfections on his head," would never die in their hearts or memory! But no more of this. The subject is too painful to dwell on; and I should be untrue to myself if 1 did not admit, that my own tears would have mingled with those shed over the grave of John Mytton, and that they have more than once mingled with the ink which has traced his devious course and marked his miserable end.

The following account of the funeral appeared in the Shrewsbury Chronicle:—

"FUNERAL OF
THE LATE JOHN MYTTON, Esq.

"We last week announced the death of this gentleman. His body was conveyed from London, where he expired, to this town, with all solemnity. On passing through the town, many of the shops were closed; and crowds assembled to take a last look on his bier, and pay the homage of a sigh to the memory of John Mytton. We rejoice to say that, before his death the consolations of religion had been eagerly resorted to, and afforded him both comfort under affliction, and hope in the prospect of eternity.

"A hearse with four horses (driven by an attached servant of the deceased), a mourning coach and four, and another carriage formed the melancholy cavalcade through Shrewsbury. On the road to Oswestry, every mark of respect was paid; and at the Queen's Head, the corpse was met by a detachment of the North Shropshire Cavalry (of which regiment the deceased was Major) who escorted them to the vault in the Chapel of Halston, where the remains were deposited at three o'clock on Wednesday afternoon. The procession was exceedingly well arranged under the direction of Mr. Dunn, of London, assisted by Messrs. Hanmer and Gittins, of this town, and entered the domain of Halston in the following order :—

Four Trumpeters of the North Shropshire Cavalry
Capt. Croxon and Capt. Jones.
Thirty-two Members of the Cavalry.
A Standard of the Regiment covered with Crape.
Forty-two Members of the Cavalry.
Adjutant Shirley and Cornet Nicolls.
Mr. Dunn (undertaker) and Mr. Gittins.
Two Mutes.
Carriage of the Revds. W. Jones and J. D. Pigott.
Two Mourning Coaches and Four, with the
Pall-Bearers.

Hon. T. Kenyon.	A. W. Corbett, Esq.
R. A. Slaney, Esq., M.P.	J. R. Kynaston, Esq
J. C. Pelham, Esq.	Rev. H. C. Cotton.

The Hearse, drawn by Four Horses, with

LIFE OF MYTTON

THE BODY,

In a Coffin covered with Black Velvet, with massive Handles richly ornamented, the Plate inscribed

'JOHN MYTTON, Esq. of HALSTON,
' Born 30th of Sept., 1796,
' Died 29th of March, 1834.'

(The Hearse was driven by Mr. Bowyer, the Deceased's Coachman, who, with Mr. M'Dougal, another Servant, attended him in his last moments).
Mourning Coach with two Mourners, the Rev. E. H. Owen (Deceased's Uncle), and the Hon. and Rev. R. Noel Hill.
Mrs. Mytton's Carriage.
Lady Kynaston's Carriage, with Mr. W. H. Griffiths and Mr. Cooper.
Carriage of A. W. Corbett, Esq.
Carriage of the Rev. Sir Edward Kynaston, Bart.
Carriage of the Rev. E. H. Owen.
Carriage of R. A. Slaney, Esq., M.P.
Carriage and Four of the Hon. Thomas Kenyon.
J. Beck, Esq., in his Carriage.
Dr. Cockerill and Lieut. Tudor, in Carriage.
Carriage of T. N. Parker, Esq.
Carriage of W. Ormsby Gore, Esq., M.P.
Carriage of the Viscountess Avonmore,
Several Cars, &c., with friends.
Mr. Broughall, Agent.

About One Hundred of the Tenantry, Tradesmen, and Friends on Horseback, closed the procession. Among these were Messrs. Longueville, Cartwright, Bolas, Hughes, J. Howell, S. Windsor, J. Williams, Morris, Griffiths, Venables, D. Thomas, W. Francis, R. Edwards, Farr, Blandford, Rogers, Davies, &c. &c.

The Mutes were old men, brothers, John and Edward Niccolas, of Whittington; the latter was mute at the funeral of the deceased's grandfather; John was mute at the grandfather's funeral, the father's funeral, and at that of Mr. Mytton.

"A mourning peal was rung at Oswestry, and the bells of Shrewsbury, Ellesmere, Whittington, Halston, &c., tolled during the day. The number of spectators was immense, and the road along which the procession slowly moved was bedewed with the tears of thousands who wished to have a last glance. Everything was conducted with the greatest order; but there was a great rush to enter the chapel on the body being taken out of the hearse. The body was placed in a shelf in the family vault, under the communion table of Halston Chapel, surrounded by the coffins of twelve of his relatives"

The family of Mytton, as has already been shown, is an ancient one; and the inhabitants of Shropshire and Wales are attached to it from many old historical, personal, and feudal recollections. Halston is called in ancient deeds *Haly Stone* or *Holy Stone*. Near it stood the abbey, taken down above a century ago. Meyric Lloyd, Lord of some part of Uch Ales, in the reign of Richard I. would not yield subjection to the English government, under which the hundred of Dyffryn Clwyd, and several others were then; and having taken some English officers that came there to execute the law, killed several of them. For this fact he forfeited his lands to the king; fled, and *took sanctuary* at Halston, where he was taken to the protection of its possessor, John Fitzalen, Earl of Arundel. In the Saxon era, the lordship of Halston belonged to Edrio; at which time there were on it two Welchmen and one Frenchman. After the Norman Conquest, Halston became the property of an Earl of Arundel, and was given by that family to the Knights of St. John of Jerusalem.—In the 26th of Henry VIII. the commandry was valued at £160 14*s.* 10*d.* a year. Upon the abolition of many of the military religious orders, Henry VIII. empowered John Sewster, Esq. to dispose of this manor to Alan Horde, who made an exchange with Edward Mytton, Esq. of Habberley; which alienation was afterwards confirmed by Queen Elizabeth. The church or chapel of Halston, is a donative, without any other revenue than what the chaplain is allowed by the owner, and is exempt of jurisdiction. Halston was the birth-place of the famous General Mytton.

Immediately after the funeral his last will was read, in which he had bequeathed all that he had to leave equally amongst all his children, and to which the Hon. Thomas Kenyon, of Pradoe, near Oswestry, and R. A. Slaney, Esq., M.P. for Shrewsbury, were appointed executors. He had previously, at Calais, made a will to which Sir Edward Smythe, Mr. Owen, of Woodhouse, Shropshire (his uncle), and myself, were appointed executors, in which his *all* was left to his only child by his first wife. The alteration, however, was immaterial, his "all," poor fellow, that is to say, his disposable personal property, being nothing; but it is consoling to think that estates amounting to £4,500 per annum were out of his reach, by entail, and still remain to his family. Thus is it possible, that by the aid of a ten years' minority, and, *barring another "John Mytton,"* Halston and its oaks[1] may yet flourish. The heir-apparent, now in his fourteenth year, is at Eton school.

One question may very naturally be asked— Why was not that substitute for the law of Corinth, the High Court of Chancery appealed to, to endeavour to stop the final dissipation of the unentailed portion of this fine property, since it is quite evident that for the last several years the unfortunate proprietor was not equal to the management of it—no, not more so than a child of six years old? This question is answered in

[1] It has been stated to me, that the amount of timber sold by Mr. Mytton at various times was £80,000, but I will not pledge myself to the fact

many ways. Mr. Mytton's nearest connexions were compelled, early in life, to leave him to his fate, their endeavours to save him from ruin having been always rejected by himself. He would not, like Savage, spurn the friend who presumed to dictate to him, but he heeded him not. That he was half mad without drink, and rendered quite mad with it, no man who knew him latterly can for a moment doubt; and a waggon load of evidence could be produced to prove that fact. But let us suppose a commission of inquiry, a writ *de Lunatico inquirendo* to have been issued! Why the result would have been this:—he would have kept himself sober for two days, and, like Sophocles before the Areopagus, would have dumb-founded his opponents. I am, however, quite certain that from the time he arrived first at Calais to the day of his death, bordering on three years, he had not the slightest insight into his own pecuniary affairs, nor did he know, to thousands, how he stood in the world; and moreover, if he had had ten thousand pounds put into his hands any one day, he would not have had a shilling of it left by that day week!! I can bring a host of evidence to back me in this assertion; and it was in vain that his friends asked him to call for something like a statement of his cash account from those who received his purchase money, for estates sold for upwards of fifty thousand pounds, subsequently to his arrival in Calais.

Having now traced this extraordinary character —this anomaly in human nature—this mixture of very right and very wrong—this strange compound of contradictory qualities — through the various stages of his eventful life, over which he may be said to have posted with the rapidity with which he travelled on the road, or, rather, with which he crossed a country after his hounds, knocking down everything before him, I shall bring his memoir to an end; and if I have followed him through a long train of errors or follies, which mark his eventful course, it has not been for the purpose of exposing but of accounting for them. If I have bared the sore with one hand I have endeavoured to find a balm for it with the other, and it would be needless to demand of me—"who hath required this at your hands?" I had the concurrence of those most nearly and dearly connected with him, one of whom observed, with no less feeling than truth, that the task I have undertaken would "do the living service and rescue the character of the dead." The man himself has passed away, yet his good deeds remain; as to his follies, we will cast them to the winds; but unfortunately for his character when alive, as well as for his memory now he is no more,

> "There is a lust in man, no charm can tame,
> Of loudly publishing his neighbour's shame:
> On eagle's wings immortal scandals fly,
> While virtuous actions are but born and die."

He has been represented as a monster for acts he has never committed, and why should the sun be thus permitted — and "falsely thus" — to go down upon his shame? It is true, there is one mournful blemish on his character which, as has already been said, I wish could be washed in Lethe and forgotten, as I can offer no extenuation for it but insanity. But if I have given the lie to one single calumny which an illnatured world has cast upon the late John Mytton *unjustly*, I shall be satisfied. He is the best man, says one of the best judges of mankind, that has the fewest faults; but he that has none is not to be found on this earth.[1] Poor Mytton's faults were the faults of the head, not of the heart, than which no man had a sounder or a kinder. They were numerous, I admit; but let not their number be augmented, neither let his many virtues be forgotten—and above all, remember the years in which he suffered adversity!

---

[1] Vitiis nemo sine nascitur; optimus ille
Qui *minimis* urgetur.—Hor.

This part of his history, however, cannot be without a useful moral. The contemplation of distress, no matter how created, corrects the pride of prosperity, softens the mind of man, and makes the heart better. Indeed, it was by such representations to the public eye that the nature of man was first polished and refined.[1]

The service done to the living only commences here. By pointing out the fatal rock on which Mr. Mytton struck, a beacon is erected which might warn others—if they would see it—who are entering now on the voyage of life, and the vicissitudes of his latter days and the melancholy circumstances of his death are fearful lessons to the present possessors of

[1] I one day told Mr. Mytton, in jest, I should write a history of his life, if I survived him. "I shall write it myself," he replied, "like Antoninus's καθ ἑαυτόν!" It will be remembered that, in a frolic, I did write his epitaph some years since at Halston, and it was, I am sorry to say, prophetic. It ran thus :—

" Here lies John Mytton; his short career is past,
The pace was quick, and therefore could not last,
From end to end he went an arrant burst,
Determined to be nowhere, or be first.
No marble monument proclaims his fate—
No pompous emblems of funereal state;
But let this simple tablet say,
That, upon a much lamented day,
There went to ground, beneath this mould'ring sod,
An honest man—the noblest work of God."

what he once was master of—namely, *all that might make life desirable and happy.* That memorable position then, that good is often the consequence of evil, is once more illustrated ; and, as the poet says, it often happens, when they little dream of it, that

> " The sons of men may owe
> The fruits of bliss to bursting clouds of woe."

Let me indulge in a few more moral reflections, as such themes do not often present themselves to my pen. Man has been represented the miracle of nature, and truly John Mytton does not give the lie to this. Perhaps no character in modern times can be found as a parallel to his, which is on one side dark and desolate ; yet if we turn the reverse, it is not difficult to determine to which side the balance inclines. But in human nature beauty and deformity are so closely linked, that in my opinion the character of no man can be very nicely weighed. Not only are there vices and virtues which bear so strong a resemblance to each other, that it is not easy to determine where the former end and where the latter begin ; but the virtues of some men are so obscured by their vices, and the vices of others so softened down by their virtues (as in both respects was the case here) that it is next to impossible to separate the chaff and cockle from the good grain. As

LIFE OF MYTTON

for reconciling the contradictions and inconsistencies we have now been recounting, it would be vain to attempt it, unless, as Johnson, with his usual force, says, "by those inconsistencies which folly produces and infirmity suffers in the human mind." At all events, an analysis of such a character as that now in our view can only be effected by a sort of debtor and creditor account of good and evil, holding the balance with a charitable hand. But it must be said of Mytton, what Clarendon said of Cromwell, and what had been said of another more than a thousand years back, that his enemies (if he had any) could not condemn him without commending him at the same time. His cardinal virtue was benevolence of heart; his besetting sin, a destroying spirit, not amenable to any counsel, and an apparent contempt for all moral restraint. In fact, like Charles the Fifth, who impiously asserted "there was but one Charles and one God," Mytton appeared to aim at similar notoriety, and every man pays a dear price for that. To a prodigality of heart, he added a prodigality of hand which no such fortune as his could suffice, and I am very much of Tom Penn's opinion, that "if he had had two hundred thousand a year he would have been in debt in five years." But although his extravagance might have reduced Mr. Mytton to want, he would have remained a man of unblemished integrity in rags, and nothing would have engaged him in dishonest practices. Oh, no! He had a spirit, which, it is true, was "marred in its beauty," but, in this respect, never forgetful of its own nobleness. He was faithful to his friends, an indulgent landlord, and a most kind master; and, last but not least in the novelty, with all this consideration for the happiness of others, he appears to have possessed very little for himself.

But he is now—ill-fated man—safe in his urn, and let no one attempt to throw more stones at his monument. There are specks in the sun, straggling weeds amongst the choicest flowers; and until the sons of Adam cease to be the sons of Adam, perfection must not be expected from them. From a retrospect of his career, let this moral be drawn:—Life has been compared to wine; *it must not be drawn to the dregs*: and all who may have it in their power, as he had, to drain nature to satiety, will find out at last—as I myself have at last found out—that tranquillity of mind and health of body, which form the happiness as well as the security of life, are not to be enjoyed under the tyrant rule of passion, and *nowhere* without something like discretion to guide and direct us in our ordinary concerns and pursuits.

PART IV

AS may be supposed, the first edition of the Life of Mr. Mytton in the form of a book, as well as its first appearance in the pages of the New Sporting Magazine, created considerable interest in the county of Salop; it also gave rise to the recalling to mind other adventures and hair-breadth escapes of this most extraordinary man, besides such as I had already detailed. Some of these I am now about to add to them have presented themselves to my recollection since the Memoir was written, and others are from a quarter—and those by far the greater part—which I have good reason to believe may be considered a sufficient guarantee for the truth of them. They have been sent me by the writer of the interesting papers contributed, under the name of "Junglicus," (who, it appears, is a native of Shropshire,) to the pages of the New Sporting Magazine. Suppose then, I commence with a few more of his larking exploits on horseback, and in carriages, in which perhaps no man yet born was his equal.[1]

On one occasion, on his return from hunting, and when within a couple of miles of Halston, he laid a trifling wager with one of the party who accompanied him, that he would reach home, the first. He suffered his friend to take the lead until they arrived on the Halston domain, and were going at speed in a line with the lake, which is one of considerable breadth; when, suddenly pulling up his horse, and forcing him into the water, he was conveyed by him with safety across it. Thus, by cutting off an acute angle, he gained a considerable advantage over his competitor; and, jumping the sunken fence into the flower garden, arrived first at his hall door. It must be observed that Mr. Mytton could not swim, even a little—not across a duck pond!

It has already been shown how regardless Mr. Mytton was of weather, whether hot or cold; and with the

[1] I am certain it will be considered but fair towards myself to state here, that when this Memoir appeared in the pages of the New Sporting Magazine, I never contemplated its coming forth in the shape of a book, illustrated with plates, and not having an opportunity of revising the press, some errors unavoidably crept in, which it has now been in my power to correct.

thermometer at zero, he would be seen walking to his stables before breakfast, with nothing on his person but his shirt, dressing gown, and slippers. On one occasion he mounted a hunter in this partial attire, and, accompanied by one of his guests, equally wild as himself, rode bare-backed over the country for three or four miles. In some of these frolics, however, he ascertained the good properties of his horses, with which perhaps he would not otherwise have been acquainted. For example —at the end of a capital run, in Shropshire, his whipper-in rode a horse called Oliver, over a brook which Mytton's own horse refused. "Stop," said he to him; "it is fit that the master should ride the *best* horse;" and from that day till he became blind, which was not for several seasons afterwards, no person but himself rode Oliver with hounds.

Frolics of all sorts delighted him. On one occasion a thought struck him that a good race might be made between waggon horses; and seeing four of his own at the moment, he ordered all their gearing, except their bridles, to be taken off them, and to be drawn up in a line. Having mounted one of them himself, he persuaded three of his friends to jockey the others, and away they went as fast as words and blows could avail. By a preconcerted plan, however, Mytton placed the waggoner at a spot where the ground was somewhat on the descent, with orders to cry out "Who-ho," at a signal given by himself. The horses knowing the voice, and glad to obey the word, stopped so suddenly as to occasion two of his three friends, who rode on the bare back, to glide from their seats, and fall headlong to the ground.

In a long frost, Mytton was often at a loss for out of door *sport*, although he was far from being particular as to the means by which it could be procured—so little so indeed that I remember his once letting out a fox, and a lot of his own hounds to hunt him, when he was aware that no horseman —not even himself—had a chance to follow them over two fields, and consequently they were seen no more till the next morning. Being, however, during one very hard frost, quite at a loss for a lark, he had recourse to the following expedient. He sent to Oswestry for twenty pairs of skates, and had twenty of his servants (stable-boys, &c.) mounted upon them, the greater part of them, as may be supposed, for the first time in their lives. He then had a number of rats turned down before terriers—one of each at a time—on the ice, when tumbling was the order of the day. But a circumstance occurred which put a stop to the diversion, if such it could be called; and I only wonder that the person who was the cause of it escaped with whole bones. The purveyor of the rats was the cowherd, who was paid *by the tails* for his rats on all other occasions, and to ensure payment for these, had actually cut off their tails before turning them down, which Mytton accidentally found out by seeing blood upon the ice. As may be supposed, he immediately put a stop to such a barbarous proceeding, and had not the old cowherd been a favourite, he would have had an awful beating.

I have already stated that there was a heronry at Halston, in which there were annually from fifty to eighty nests. Mytton expressed a wish to have some young herons taken in order to satisfy himself of the asserted superiority of heron over rook pie. The nests being on the very tops of high trees, neither his keepers, nor any persons about the house, would undertake to get them. "Here goes then," said Mytton; and stripping off his coat and waistcoat, he ascended a tree of prodigious height, and safely brought down his prize.

Whilst in the Seventh Hussars, and quartered with

the army of occupation in France, he heard of a badger that no dog in that country was able to draw. Having offered a bet, which was accepted, that *he would produce a dog in a certain given time that would perform that act,* he very coolly ordered his favourite servant ("old John," as he always called him, and who was in his service from his boyhood), to go to a village called Cockshut, in Shropshire, and purchase and bring to him, one Burroughs's dog. Nor did the order end here. "If Burroughs won't part with his dog," said Mytton, "bring him over, dog and all, at his own price"! The dog, however, was bought for eight pounds, and drew the badger in great style. He was a small animal, half bull, half terrier; and having been brought to England by Mytton, remained at Halston, where he was well taken care of, till he died.

Most of his frolics were of a ludicrous at the same time of a perfectly harmless nature. I can enumerate a few. On going into the bar of the Lion Inn, Shrewsbury, one evening, when somewhat "sprung" by wine, he was told there was a box in the coach-office for him, which contained two brace of foxes. He requested it might be brought to him; when taking up the poker, he knocked off the lid of it, and let the foxes out in the room in which the landlady and some of her female friends were assembled—giving a thrilling view-holloa at the time. Now it cannot be said they "broke cover" in good style; but it may safely be asserted, that they broke such a great quantity of bottles, glasses, and crockery-ware, as to have rendered the joke an expensive one.

In 1829, having been disappointed by a blank day with Sir Edward Smythe's hounds, which then hunted the Shrewsbury country, he was determined upon a lark when he got home. He accordingly ordered some drafted hounds, which he had in his kennel at Halston, together with all the terriers and bull-dogs, about the house, to be taken to a certain place, where he also ordered to be assembled all the servants of his establishment, mounted on whatever they could catch—such as ponies, donkeys, or mules—and a fox to be turned out before them. The scene was, as may be supposed, a most ludicrous one, although it was accidentally concluded by an act of cruelty from which humanity revolts. A stable-boy, on a fast pony, having been first up when the fox was laid hold of by the hounds, cut off his brush without waiting for him to be killed, and, breaking away from the park, the poor animal ran over several fields in that mutilated state before he was again run into by the pack. But Mytton was often in the habit of mounting his servants with his hounds when he turned out bag foxes, merely for the sake of witnessing the falls they got, from their want of skill in horsemanship. And he was equally fond of creating amusement, even at the expense of his own person. For example:—During his successful contest for the borough of Shrewsbury, in 1819, he threw himself from the car in which he was being carried home from the hustings, through a window into the Lion Inn in that town, at the imminent hazard of his life. But the turmoil of a contested election was a fine field for John Mytton. On one occasion the principal champion of the opposing party stood opposite to his inn, challenging *any man* to contend with him. Mytton listened to his bravado for a while; till his Welch blood being excited; when he set to and thrashed him to his heart's content after only five rounds. He then put something into his fist, as he said, "to make him comfortable for the evening."

He was very much beloved by the labouring classes within a large circle round his house, and would occasionally enter their cottages without invitation or ceremony. His horse having fallen with him one day, and broken his knees very badly, he applied to an old woman by the road side, for some linen bandages to apply to them. Being unable to furnish them, he thus addressed her. "Never mind, my good woman; bring your scissors here and cut off the tail of my shirt, and then you may cut up the sleeves of it, which will make capital bandages." On another occasion, after having been long exposed to cold on the Hawkestone hills, with hounds, he entered a house near Wem, taking his favourite hunter, Baronet, along with him; and having ordered a good fire to be made to warm himself *and his horse*, departed for home, saying they were both very much the better for it, and also for what they found in the house,—for he was by no means particular as to what he helped himself or his horse on these occasions; and is said once to have seriously injured a horse by dosing him as he dosed himself—*with wine*.[1]

Again—he one day rode *at* the Ellesmere canal, and of course got a ducking. Finding himself very cold, on the road home, with his hounds, he exchanged his wet coat for a flannel petticoat which he espied on a cottager's garden hedge; and slipping it over his

[1] It is stated by a correspondent that the horse I allude to, called Sportsman, dropped down dead in his gig, in consequence of his owner having given him a bottle of mulled port wine at Wrexham. I knew the horse well, but cannot vouch for the cause of his death.

head, pursued his course, to the great amusement of all spectators, leaving his coat to be brought to Halston by the owner of the said petticoat!

In speaking of Mr. Mytton as a horseman, I have stated the singular fact of his never having so completely tired his horses in the field as to have been obliged to walk home, which I, in great part, attribute to his strength of hand in assisting them in their work. It is true he rode excellent horses, for bad ones were useless to him; but he really appeared to have a sort of magic influence over their tempers — at all events it seemed as if they sympathised with him in his frolics—for they were always tranquil under him, and would do almost any thing he required them to do. He would ride them up steps, and down steps, and round the inside of the house, without their appearing to be in the least disconcerted or alarmed, nor did I ever hear that he was a sufferer by such dangerous frolics.

Some of Mytton's practical jokes were rather "beyond a joke"—or in other words, he would sometimes "drive the jest too far." For example. He had the wire of a spring gun laid in the path, in his shrubbery at Halston, which he knew his chaplain would take on his road to church. So soon as he heard the report, for which he was of course on the watch, he ran out of the house and accused the parson *of shooting at his pheasants on a Sunday.* His reverence's nerves, however, were so disturbed by the shock, that he was unable to face his congregation until he returned to the house and composed himself. Mytton's universal remedy was proposed by him, and two glasses of Madeira made the parson all right again.

Mytton may be said to have lived in a storm, for a row was his delight. Nevertheless, although there was an apparent ferocity of temper about him at times, it was blended with much kindness of heart, and he scarcely ever thrashed a man that he did not give him something afterwards as amends. I remember hearing of an unfortunate horsebreaker having been carried, *nolens volens,* by a half-broken colt into the midst of his hounds. Mytton flogged him severely, and then gave him a guinea. But there are scores of similar facts to this upon record — one of which I have already related. He would not, however, suffer any man to take an improper liberty with him, and, in that case, there was no compensation for a thrashing. A Shrewsbury tradesman, when a little "sprung" ventured to call him "Johnny." Mytton floored him on the spot.

He was the dread of the owners of the minor gambling-tables who frequent country races, for he was given to break their banks in more ways than one. In the first place, as I before observed, he was often a great winner; and in the next, he would demolish the entire apparatus if he suspected any unfair advantage to be taken of himself, or of any other person in the room. At Warwick races, in 1824, he and his companions not only broke a rouge et noir table to atoms, but gave the proprietor of it and his gang a sound drubbing into the bargain. They applied to the magistrates for redress, but Mytton had been beforehand with them, and consequently they got none. He was likewise once, together with some others, surprised by the Mayor of Chester, in the act of playing hazard, in a room hired for the purpose, on the *Sunday evening* previous to the races of that town. On seeing the Mayor enter, he coolly put his winnings into his hat; then the hat on his head; and then walked away unnoticed, being taken only for a spectator.

I have spoken of Mytton as a shot, and I believe no *sportsman* need be superior to what he was at one time of his life. For myself, I only knew him as a game shot, as the term is, never having seen him with

Drawn and Etched by T. J. Rawlins and H. Alken

A b-ll of a row in a hall... Neptune shows fight.

either pistol or rifle in his hand. It has, however, been represented to me, on the authority to which I have before alluded, that he was a most superior marksman with a rifle—so superior indeed as to be able to hit the edge of a razor at a distance of thirty yards, and occasionally to split his ball! "*Credat Judæus*"—I do not add "*non ego*"; yet I never chanced to hear of such a wonderful performance. But I will transcribe the rest of the story, and leave my readers to make the best of it.

"He would," writes my informant, "cross the yard (at Halston), and shoot from one of the iron gates on the drive, or carriage road, to the coal-house wall, a distance of fifty-five yards, and put his ball through the peg-hole of a trimmer (used for pike fishing). The trimmer-cork, in this instance, was placed on the tame fox's cub, or kennel, with the flat side towards Mytton's aim; and it invariably fell to the ground on each time of being fired at,—the ball actually going through the aperture where the peg of the trimmer is put in, and not above an inch and a half diameter, covered with a piece of white paper, pasted thereon, to ascertain the fact. This he has done over and over again to the amazement of all who have witnessed it, and with his rifle *to his shoulder*, and not on a *rest*, as might be imagined by some. Talk of Americans, for their precision in shooting, after this! It cannot be surpassed, if equalled." To this account is added the fact of his having shot rats with a rifle, from the top of his house, and sundry other achievements, rather too marvellous to relate.[1]

As I have already said, no part of this extraordinary man's character is more interesting to the generality of the readers of this memoir, than that which relates to his exploits in the saddle and in carriages.

During the period of Sir Bellingham Graham hunting Shropshire, he performed several gallant feats in the field. Whilst suffering severely from the effects of a fall, and with his right arm in a sling, he rode his favourite hunter, Baronet, over the park paling of the late Lord Berwick, of Atsham, near Shrewsbury, to the astonishment of the whole field — Sir Bellingham himself exclaiming, "Well done, Neck or Nothing; you are not a bad one to breed from." With the same hounds, he signalized himself greatly in a run from Bomer-wood to Haughmond-hill, when the river Severn brought the field to check.

---

[1] For example.—He is *represented* as having more than once put a ball through a man's hat, whilst on his head!

Drawn and Etched by T. J. Rawlins

Mytton swims the Severn at Uphampton Ferry
"He that calls himself a Sportsman, let him follow me."

LIFE OF MYTTON

Three or four of them managed to get their horses into a boat, but Mytton scorned its assistance. "Let all who call themselves sportsmen," he exclaimed, "follow me;" and, dashing into the stream, gained the opposite bank, and was one of the very few who saw the fox killed. It must again be observed, that Mytton was no swimmer, and the Severn is broad and deep, and with banks none of the best.

On another occasion, he nearly lost his life in the Severn, in a run with his own hounds, near Bridgenorth. All the field but himself crossed it by a horse-ferry boat, but he gallantly plunged into it, although it was much swollen by rain at the time. His mare—a fine hunter, called Cara Sposa —was carried a long way down the stream by the current, and although she at length gained the opposite side with him, the bank would not admit of her landing herself. His whipper-in (Ned Evans), however, who had crossed by the boat, fortunately came to his assistance, and pulled him up the bank, leaving the mare in the water. Nor does the story end here. Jumping upon the whip's mare, Mytton got to his hounds, and the mare was eventually brought ashore, without much injury.

Still I have reason to believe the hair-breadth

escapes on wheels even exceeded those in the saddle, which perhaps may be in some measure accounted for by his early predilection for tandem driving— the most hazardous of any, even in the best of hands, and Mytton was no coachman.[1] The following feat, if true, certainly out-herod's Herod; but my readers shall have it exactly as I myself had it, accompanied with the following remark;—Nothing, we are led to believe is impossible with God; nothing was improbable of the late John Mytton.

"He was one day," says my informant, "engaged to dine with a friend at some distance from Halston, and came, as usual, in his tandem. After dinner, the conversation turning on the danger of that mode of harnessing horses, from the little command the driver can have over the leader, Mytton at once expressed his dissent from this doctrine; and being under the influence of the "rosy god," offered to bet a pony (£25) all round, that he would, *that night*, drive his tandem across the country, into the turnpike road, a distance of half a mile, having in his progress to get over a sunk-fence, three yards wide; a broad deep

---

[1] When I say he was "no coachman," I mean he knew nothing of the science or system of driving four horses. He would, however, now and then take hold of a team in the Holyhead mail, and I was told that when he did, he never attempted to *lark*.

Drawn and Etched by T. J. Rawlins and H. Alken

How to enjoy a country comfortably after dinner.

drain; and two stiff quick-set-fences, with ditches on the further side!! The bets offered were taken by several of the party present, to the tune of £150 and upwards, and after the necessary preparations, all turned out to see the fun, although in justice it should be said, as Mytton was then under age, it was not only proposed to him that the bets made should be off, but he was strongly persuaded not to make the attempt. This, however, with him had always a contrary effect; and twelve men, with lanthorns on poles, having been procured, to aid the light of the moon, away went Mytton at the appointed signal being given.

"The first obstacle was the sunk fence, *into* which, as may be expected, he was landed; but the opposite side being on a gradual slope, from bottom to top, the carriage and its extraordinary inmate, by dint of whipping, were drawn out without receiving injury. Nowise disconcerted, he sent his team at the next fence—the wide drain—and such was the pace he went at, that it was cleared by a yard or more; but the jerk pitched Mytton on the wheeler's back; but crawling over the dashing leather, he resumed his seat, and got his horses again into the proper direction, and taking the two remaining fences in gallant style, got safe into the turnpike road, and pocketed the cash. This occurred at Mr. Walford's[1] of Cronkhill, about four miles from Shrewsbury."

The above appears somewhat of a miraculous adventure; but that Mytton was equal to the attempt, no one who knew him as well as I knew him would doubt. Indeed I have already stated a fact (I think in my Shropshire Tour) bearing some relation to it. He was driving me from Shrewsbury to Chillington to dinner, and after one or two trifling occurrences, such as knocking down a bullock, and breaking a shaft of the gig on the road, we found ourselves in an awkward predicament. By having taken a wrong turn, on approaching the house, we found ourselves in a field with no means of getting out of it, except by the gate by which we entered it; and we were already behind time for dinner. "We'll manage it," said Mytton; "*this horse is a capital fencer*, so do you get over the fence (a hedge and ditch) and catch him." He then merely unbuckled the bearing rein, gave the horse a cut with his whip, and over he came, gig and all, without the slightest accident.

[1] I knew Mr. Walford, and, for all that I know to the contrary, he is alive to refute or confirm this statement.

Amongst the numerous anecdotes sent to me since the publication of the first edition of this memoir, was the following. Having shown a friend his entire stud at Halston, as also his hounds, &c., he told him he had something still better worth his seeing, in reserve for him; and on opening his coach-house doors, he thus addressed him. "You see that gig; last night it was carried clean over my lodge gate, and it is not a bit the worse for it, nor, as you have seen, is the horse that carried it over." Now this sounds rather marvellous; but the inhabitants of the town of Wrexham, in Denbighshire, can well remember a somewhat similar circumstance occurring at a villa close to that town, some twenty years back. A horse, the property of the late Mr. Watkin Hayman, ran away with his gig from the door, and carried it over a high palisade gate, without injury to either himself or the gig. I went the next day to see the gate, and the only impression left upon it was the fracture of one of the spikes, or points, of the top rail. But Mytton would wantonly seek accidents from gigs and phaetons; and, latterly, I never entered into one with him, but on condition of his having nothing to do with the reins. I remember seeing him get out of his phaeton at the hall door at Halston, and instead of letting a servant drive it round to the stables, start the horses off by themselves, at a gallop; and, strange to say, they conducted the carriage safely into the yard, although they had two rather sharp turns to make, and one gate to go through. This was in the life-time of the first Mrs. Mytton, who had more than one providential escape from this same phaeton.

In his love of frolics, I never knew nor heard of but one person anywise his equal. This was the late well known "Tom Leigh," as he was generally called, of High Leigh, in Cheshire, a gentleman of very large fortune, and altogether a truly singular character. He had a regular pit-fall in his grounds, into which he would walk a stranger who came to visit him, and sundry other manœuvres which he called sport. Even the parson of the parish was not exempt from being made the subject of a lark, as the following anecdote will show. Imagining himself to be a good judge of horse-flesh, he invariably brought his new purchase to the Squire of High Leigh, partly for his approbation, and partly in proof of his own skill in the selection of him. On one occasion the nag was ordered into the stable, and his reverence also well taken care of for the night, the next morning being a hunting morning. "Now Doctor," said the Squire, as soon as breakfast was over, "we will go into the stables and see this famous new horse of yours, of which you have talked to me so much." But he was not to be found. The parson declared he himself put him in a particular stall; and *there in truth he was;* but the Squire having ordered him to be cropped and docked over night, his owner had not the slightest recollection of him. As may be supposed, a hearty laugh was raised at his expense, and there was an end of all future, somewhat boring, exhibitions of inferior animals to a man who had some of the best horses that money could procure, and who was really a judge of them. But I was never an admirer of practical jokes, especially when, as in this instance, the sufferings of an animal form a feature in them. Neither were many of the frolics of poor Mytton creditable to him. In the first place they are always inconsistent with manhood; and in the next, knowing no bounds with him, they often led him into excesses which endangered his character as a man, and verified the censure passed upon them by Horace:—

> " Lusit amabiliter; donec jam sævus apertam
> In rabiem verti cœpit jocus."

Some idea may be formed of Mr. Mytton's zeal in the pursuit of every description of sporting, by the following extract from the catalogue of effects sold at Halston, when the establishment was broken up.

NET HOUSE.

Three bush nets, 26 and 28 yards long, 5 deep
Two small mesh nets for bushes
Three larger ditto ditto
Two drag nets, with large tunnels
Four trammel flue nets of various sizes
One minnow net
One minnow net and pole
Three gutter nets. Two casting nets
Two drum nets. One cleaching net
One large salmon net
One gudgeon, or fine meshed, brook net
Four landing nets of various sizes
Six fishing poles   Four bait cans
Two large fish cans. Two angling chairs
Two coracles, or small fishing boats
Two eel spears. Two trout spears
One salmon spear. Fishing cases and rods of every description.

IN THE ENGINE HOUSE AND AVIARY

Six pheasant nets
Three rabbit nets and several purse nets
Two pairs of lark nets
One partridge net
Various rabbit traps, in lots
One hundred and twenty-eight vermin traps of every description
One badger cub
Two fox cubs
Thirteen dog kennels
Fourteen ferret boxes
Three cages for wild animals
Nine bird cages
Sixteen pairs of quoits
Two sets of bowls
Sundry cricket bats and balls

Drawn and Etched by T. J. Rawlins and H. Alken

Heavy Shooting : "A cooler, after a hup drunk."

GUNS.

Six rifles of various bores
Nine double-barrelled guns
Four single ditto
Some dozens of powder flasks
Shot belts, Gun cases, &c. &c.

As a finish to his shooting career, the following anecdote may be relied upon. On a very cold morning after a very *warm* night, he disturbed some herons, whilst pheasant shooting. "They are out of distance, sir," said his keeper. "The devil they are!" replied Mytton; "but I'll be with them," and into the water he plunged.

Perhaps Mytton never made himself much more conspicuous in the field, than he did upon what, a few years back, was well known in the hunting circles of Cheshire, Shropshire, and Staffordshire, as "The Shavington Day." This was a day on which a trial of speed, nose, and bottom was to be made between the fox-hounds of Sir Harry Mainwaring, of Peover-Hall, Cheshire, commonly called "the Cheshire hounds," hunted by Will Head, now huntsman to the Marquis of Hastings; those kept jointly by Sir Edward Smythe, of Acton Burnal-park, Mr. Smythe Owen, of Condoverhall, and Mr. Lloyd, of Aston-hall, each in the County of Salop, (late Sir Bellingham Graham's) commonly called "the Shropshire hounds"; and those of Mr. Wicksted, whose kennel is at Betley, near Newcastle-under-Lyne, from which they hunt what is called "the Woore country," once hunted by the late Sir Thomas Mostyn, previously to his taking Oxfordshire, and likewise a part of Shropshire; hunted by Charles Wells, formerly huntsman to the Oakley, in the time of Lords Ludlow and Tavistock, and who is still, I believe, with Mr. Wicksted. The interest taken, for many surrounding miles, in this extraordinary, and, I believe I may add, *unique* undertaking, was immense; and it was supposed that, independently of the contents of carriages, there were considerably more than a thousand horsemen in the field, about seven hundred of them clad in scarlet.

Mytton, as usual, was resolved to make himself conspicuous in more ways than one on this memorable occasion; and on the preceding evening he arrived at Whitchurch, to be near to the scene of action, and where he had ordered the best dinner that could be provided for himself and two friends, who accompanied him. But the dinner at Whitchurch and its evils, were not "sufficient for the day"; he ordered his carriage in the evening, and drove to the village of Wrenbury, the rendezvous of the different packs, and where a main of cocks was being fought. Having seen what was going on there, he returned to his quarters at Whitchurch, and after drawing a commercial traveller from his bed, and dosing him with wine, retired at length to his own.

The place of meeting to decide this important affair, was Shavington-hall, the seat of the late Viscount Kilmorey, who, although but little of a fox-hunter himself, was a great promoter of the sport, by his strict preservation of foxes; and he left an excellent name behind him, as one of "the right sort." The time fixed was eleven o'clock, and at that hour a scene highly interesting to sportsmen presented itself, and indeed to all descriptions of persons who witnessed it; for it is well known that there is nothing which adds more to scenery, fine scenery, which this park affords, than a numerously attended pack of hounds, in motion.

The modus operandi was this:—Six couples out of each pack were selected for the trial, forming a properly sized pack, and they appeared in the field, attended by their respective huntsmen, namely, Will Head, for the Cheshire; John Wrigglesworth, now huntsman to Mr. Smythe Owen, for the Shropshire;

and Charles Wells, for Mr. Wicksted's—Will Head acting as leading huntsman of the day, by reason of its being the country which his hounds claimed as their own as well as Cheshire being the senior pack.

These being the best days of the Tomkinsons, the Gleggs, the Brookes, Jack Ford, and sundry other first flight Cheshire men, it may naturally be imagined, that a spirit of rivalry amongst men would accompany the trial of speed in hounds, and that Mytton would be amongst the foremost to distinguish himself. That he came prepared to do so, was evident by the fact of his having had his capital Hit-or-Miss mare reserved for this particular occasion, orders having been given to his groom to " have her right fit to go." [1]

Precisely at the hour of twelve, the business of the day commenced ; the pack were thrown into what is called the Big-wood, in Shavington-park, from which a fox almost immediately broke, and, having stood

[1] Many of your readers will remember my account, in my Shropshire Tour, of this Hit-or-Miss mare having carried Mr. Mytton, superbly, throughout a capital run of an hour and forty minutes, with Sir Bellingham Graham's hounds, from Babbins-wood, and over a very severe country. Sir Bellingham confessed, that he had never before been so ridden away from, as he was on that day by Mytton, and that is saying enough for the merits of the Hit-or-Miss mare

Drawn and Etched by T. J. Rawlins and H. Alken

"A Squire-trap, by Jove, over Neptune, a little more and I should have done it."

before them for thirty minutes, at a very severe pace, was lost near the village of Clovely Mytton very soon got the lead, and very soon lost it, and nearly his life at the same time; for coming to a deep sunk fence, or ha-ha, at which there was a high and stiff rail, on the rising side, which he gallantly charged, his mare fell and gave him a severe fall, — in addition to his being much hurt by another person's horse, that had followed him, tumbling upon him, and crushing him. "Now, FOR THE HONOUR OF SHROPSHIRE," said he, when he rode at this fence, which indicated two things; First, that he considered the fence something like a stopper; and secondly, that he was determined not to be beaten by any man in the field, so long as his mare could keep on her legs. This fall, however, shook him much, and although he remounted and went on— bleeding and *bare-headed*, for his hat was too much crushed to be worth picking up, the horse that followed him having alighted on it—he was forced to content himself with following a leader for the remainder of this day.

Not satisfied with the burst, the rival hounds drew the covers in Combermere-park, the seat of Lord Combermere, and found a second fox, which took them a ring of about twelve miles, in which some excellent hunting was displayed; but it being ascertained that they were running a heavy vixen (i.e., a bitch fox, in whelp), they were whipped off without tasting blood. As to which lot of hounds bore off the palm, it would not only be invidious, but now useless to say, neither does my informant state that fact;— and, observe, reader! the foregoing account has been forwarded to me from Shropshire, for insertion, and is not the result of my own personal observation, as I was not present on the memorable occasion which gave birth to it. I have, however, reason to believe it is a true one, inasmuch as it is quite characteristic of the man.

The stables and boxes at Halston have the doors covered with a greater or less number of plates, as the shoes worn by racers are called. They are painted light blue, with white in the centre, in which are printed all the horses' names, the stakes, &c. won by them in every year up to 1827 or later. Each stake or race won, has a plate to record it, and they are arranged by half dozens in a line across the breadth of the door. The racing career of any individual horse is recorded along with others on the door

Drawn and Etched by H. Alken and T. J. Rawlins

The Shavington day Now for the honor of Shropshire a trail of wood parks, and consequently of wood hewsmen.

LIFE OF MYTTON

of the particular stable or box he once occupied, and there are nine stables and box doors covered with plates in the following order.

First set of stables,
on the door are recorded 27 Stakes in as many plates

Second	ditto	17	ditto	ditto
Third	ditto	18	ditto	ditto
Fourth	ditto	24	ditto	ditto
Fifth	ditto	5	ditto	ditto
Sixth	ditto	6	ditto	ditto
Seventh	ditto	16	ditto	ditto
Eighth	ditto	26	ditto	ditto
Ninth	ditto	26	ditto	ditto

Total 165 Stakes.

But there are many stakes not recorded on the doors, for I am told none have been entered since the year 1827.

The following horses, &c., are recorded to have won stakes, plates, and matches, to the number specified against their respective names, viz:—

		Brought forward	8
Langolee	2	Harriet Wilson	1
Singlepeeper	1	Mandeville	8
Fox-huntress	1	Ruler	2
Chance	1	Libertine	1
Sir Oliver	1	Victorine	2
Jovial	1	Mallet	4
Milo Mare	1	Whittington	14
	8		40

Brought forward 40		*Brought forward* 118	
Alexander	2	Bowsprit	1
Habberley	13	Colt by Amadis	3
Cara Spoza	2	Oswestry	6
Ashbourn	1	Ludford	4
Anti-radical	17	Geranium	3
Banker	4	Cannon-ball Filly	1
Ostrich	2	Louisa	3
Comrade	1	George the Third	1
Colt by Bustard	2	Halston	7
Euphrates	16	Sir William	4
Flexible	6	Chancellor	1
Longwaist	5	Nettle	1
Tattoo	2	Paradigm	1
Handel	2	Berghill	6
Claudius	2	Comte d'Artois	5
Paul Potter	1		165
	118		

The foregoing account has been sent to me by a Shropshire gentleman, and I have every reason to believe it to be correct.

The following lines on the death of Mr. Mytton, were added by the publisher, the author being unknown to me. Let the merits of them speak for themselves; it only remains for me to remark, that they breathe the effusions of a warm and friendly heart, and display a knowledge of the character of the man they are intended to commemorate.

A Monody

ON THE DEATH OF JOHN MYTTON, Esq.

> "The earth
> Owns no such spirit as his."
> MANFRED.

HAST thou e'er trod Italia's classic land?
Paus'd by her temples, e'en in ruins grand?
Mark'd the rude weed's obnoxious shadow thrown
O'er sculptured forms, the gods themselves might own?
Beheld vile reptiles desecrate the shrine
That pious worshippers had deem'd divine?
Heard the loud tempest give its anger tongue
Where once devotion's holy chauntings rung?
Mark'd where the dove once rear'd her peaceful brood
The hungry vulture hold his feast of blood?
If so, what felt ye at this game of fate?
Disgust or pity? fond regret or hate?
There needs no sound to tell thy proud reply,—
Thy soul's indignant answer's in thine eye!
And shall (however beautiful) a stone
Claim from our hearts all sympathy alone?
Shall the unequall'd fabric of a man,
Built upon nature's most exalted plan,

Tho' razed by tempests and by weeds defac'd,
Tho' carrion vultures have the dove displac'd,
Tho' noisome reptiles from their slimy springs
Pollute the heart's most holy, treasur'd, things—
Say, shall we coldly gaze upon this scene,
Nor mourn the loveliness that once has been?
Aye, mourn as man may mourn, but not with tears,
His age of passion thro' a life of years;
Mourn! but no tears—they honour not the grave
Of such as MYTTON was, the kind, the brave.
His was a restless soul—too wildly prone
To wear the show of vices not his own,
To mock the love his heart most dearly priz'd,
To scorn the lesson wisdom most advis'd,
And, in the maddening poison of the bowl,
Drown in one mighty draught—heart—health—
 and soul.
His was the hand most ready to bestow,
The good effected all he ask'd to know;
The friend unchang'd—the foe that scorn'd to sue,
Himself the only victim that he slew.
His vices all deformities of art,
Whilst every virtue centered in his heart.
For such we mourn—and be our grief express'd
By faults forgotten and by good confess'd!

LaVergne, TN USA
21 May 2010
183545LV00001B/94/A